BRISTOL, CONN.

TO THE BOYS AND GIRLS WHO WILL USE THIS BOOK

The history of the United States is an exciting story. It is the story of great men and women, of great struggles, and of great achievements. It is the story of the development of thirteen weak colonies into one of the most powerful nations in the world. In this book you will read all about these stirring events.

Many people have worked hard to prepare this book for you. Authors, editors, and artists have worked long hours to make this the kind of book you will understand and enjoy. We think it is different from most histories written for boys and girls your age. We know you will learn much from this book. We also believe that you will find it interesting and attractive.

The authors who wrote this book know how to write for boys and girls. You will find most of the sentences short and easy to understand. Most of the words are simple. Of course, you will find some new words, because you wish to learn new words every year. Most of the new words are explained. Some of them are explained as soon as they are used. Others are explained in the glossary at the back of the book.

We know that boys and girls like pictures, and we have given you many pictures. You can scarcely turn a page without finding a new picture. The pictures help make the book attractive. They also tell you many things. By looking at a picture you can tell what kind of clothes certain people wore, what kind of tools they used, and what kind of houses they lived in.

It is easier to understand history if you have maps showing where various people lived and where important events took place. You will find many maps in this book. Maps will tell you why people settled in certain places — near rivers, in fertile valleys — and how these people made a living.

In this book there are many questions to help you remember what you have read. Some of the questions seem more like a quiz game than questions in a school book, but if you answer them correctly you will be learning your history well. Some of the questions will help you to think, and it is very important that you learn to think correctly.

COPYRIGHT 1955 WILLIAM H. SADLIER, INC.
MANUFACTURED IN THE UNITED STATES OF AMERICA

CONTENTS

UNIT THREE: Thirteen Growing Colonies

   12. Pilgrims and Puritans Come to New England....................102
   13. People Come to the Middle Colonies............................114
   14. The Southern Colonies...124
   15. How People Lived in the English Colonies......................130

UNIT FOUR: A New Nation

   16. The French Lose Their Land in North America...................146
   17. Bad Laws Cause Trouble..156
   18. Americans Win Their Freedom...................................167

UNIT FIVE: Early Days of Our Republic

   19. The States Form a Strong Union................................178
   20. George Washington, the First President........................185
   21. Thomas Jefferson and His Friends..............................193
   22. Andrew Jackson, a Man of the People...........................209

UNIT SIX: Our Nation Grows

   23. Pathfinders to the West.......................................216
   24. Texas, the Lone-Star State....................................222
   25. California, the Golden State..................................230
   26. The Oregon Country..240
   27. New Ways to Travel in a Growing Country.......................246

UNIT SEVEN: Our Nation Remains United

   28. Slavery Divides the Nation....................................268
   29. The Civil War...280
   Index ....III–XIV

Unit Three

THIRTEEN GROWING COLONIES

Looking Into the Long Ago

Dick was on his way to the big city. He was going to visit his cousin, Mary Jean. His mother and father had just said goodbye to him as he got on the bus. Now he was looking for a seat.

Dick saw a boy about his own age looking out the window. There was an empty seat next to the boy.

"Do you mind if I sit here?" Dick asked.

The boy looked around and smiled. "Oh, no," he said. "Please do."

There was something just a little different about the way the boy talked. He did not sound exactly like the boys Dick knew. But he was very friendly. Dick liked him right away. The boy said his name was Tom.

Dick told Tom about the farm. He told Tom about his school. Then he said, "Now tell me about yourself."

"Well I have lived in Europe up until now."

"Tell me about some of the places you have seen," said Dick.

After they had talked for a while Dick said, "How long have you been in the United States?"

"About six weeks," said Tom.

Dick was puzzled. "You certainly

100

speak our language very well for being here such a short time."

Tom smiled. "I should be able to speak English rather well. You see, I am from England."

Dick was so surprised for a minute that he did not know what to say. Then he began to laugh.

"That is a good joke on me. You said you came from Europe, and I was thinking that everyone in Europe spoke a different language than ours. I forgot all about England."

Mary Jean and her father, Mr. Davis, were waiting for Dick at the bus station. As the three got into Mr. Davis's car, Dick told about the boy he had met on the bus. Then he told what he had said to the boy.

Mr. Davis laughed. "Tom must have been very polite. He could have told you that the English people had the language long before the Americans."

"Dad," said Mary Jean, "why is it that almost all Americans speak English? We learned in history that the Spaniards, French, and Dutch all owned parts of our country at one time. Why don't we speak Spanish, French, or Dutch?"

"Well," said Mr. Davis, "Spanish is spoken by the people of Mexico, Central America, and much of South America."

"In one part of Canada," said Mr. Davis, "most of the people speak French. That is because so many French people settled there. But not so many French settled in our country."

"Most of the first settlers in our part of North America must have been English," Mary Jean said.

"Yes," her father answered. "It was the thirteen English colonies that became the United States of America."

"In that history show, I was one of the Jamestown settlers," Dick said. "I guess I was one of those who brought the English language to America."

"It's true that we owe our language to the first English settlers," said Mr. Davis. "But we also owe them much more than that."

"If we owe so much to the English settlers," said Dick, "I suppose we will spend some time this year learning about them."

"I think you will," said Mr. Davis. "Well we are almost home."

"And I see Aunt Nell standing in the doorway," said Dick.

"We will be just in time for lunch," Mary Jean said, "and Mother has your favorite dessert."

"I have so many favorite desserts, I cannot imagine what it is," said Dick. "But don't tell me. I want to be surprised."

12. Pilgrims and Puritans Come to New England

Many English People Suffered for Their Religion. The soldiers are taking these people to prison.

Why do these people have to go to prison? Because the soldiers caught them going to their own church instead of going to the Church of England.

At one time almost everybody in England was a Catholic. Then a King of England left the Catholic Church. A new church was started— the Church of England. The King of England was the head of this church. Other new churches were also started. The people who belonged to all these new churches were called Protestants because they protested against the Catholic Church.

A law was passed in England that everyone must belong to the Church of England. People who tried to go to any other church were arrested. Sometimes they had to pay a fine. Sometimes they had to go to prison.

Who are the people in the picture? Perhaps they are Catholics. The Catholics knew that their Church was the One True Church.

They would not join the Church of England. The Catholics in England had to suffer much for their Faith.

Or perhaps the people in the picture are Protestants who do not belong to the Church of England. There were many different kinds of Protestants in England. The Protestants who did not belong to the Church of England also had to suffer for their religion.

Today, in our country we have freedom of religion. This means that there is no law telling us what church we must attend. No soldiers will take us to jail for going to our own church. There was no such freedom of religion in England in the 1600's and 1700's.

Many people left England and came to America. They hoped that in America they would be able to go to their own churches without being arrested.

In this chapter we shall read about the Pilgrims and the Puritans. Both the Pilgrims and the Puritans were Protestants who suffered for their religion. They left England and came to America so they could worship God in the way they thought was right.

The Pilgrims Come to America. William Bradford was one of the Protestants who did not belong to the Church of England. He lived in the village of Scrooby, in England. When William was seventeen years old, the minister of his church was arrested.

William heard some of the men talking.

"If we stay here, we shall be arrested over and over again," the men said. "We must leave England. Let's go to Holland."

William went to Holland with the others. He was about 18 years old. In Holland, he learned to be a silk weaver.

103

But the English people were not happy in Holland. In England they had been farmers. They could not buy farms in Holland, so they had to live in the big cities. They found that it was hard for them to make a living in Holland. They also found that their children were speaking Dutch instead of English. They were afraid their children would forget their English ways.

"Let's go to America," some of the people said. "There is plenty of land in America. We can start farms there. Also, we shall be able to keep our English language and our English ways."

These people were poor. They could not buy a ship or the things they needed to start a settlement. They borrowed the money from some merchants. They agreed to pay back the money after they started their farms in America.

When it was time to sail, only 35 of the people left Holland. William Bradford was one of them. It was about this time that the people were first called Pilgrims.

When the Pilgrims got to England they were joined by 67 others. These 102 people sailed from England in September, 1620. They sailed on a ship called the *Mayflower*.

The *Mayflower* sailed through many storms. At times it seemed the waves would batter the little ship to pieces. The Pilgrims were often sea-sick and cold. It took the ship 63 days to cross the Atlantic. Today, fast steamers make the same trip in four or five days.

The Pilgrims were supposed to go to Virginia. They missed Virginia and came to land farther north. This is the land that we today call Massachusetts.

A Hard Winter at Plymouth. Before they landed the Pilgrims had a meeting. The men in the party signed an agreement. This agreement is called the Mayflower Compact. The men said they would obey all the laws made for the colony. They elected John Carver to be their governor.

The Pilgrims explored the coast. They were looking for a place to build a settlement. They came to a fine harbor. Captain John Smith had discovered this harbor a few years earlier. He had named it Plymouth, after the city of Plymouth in England. The Pilgrims decided to build their settlement at Plymouth. The Pilgrims finally landed on December 10, 1620. They knelt and thanked God for a safe landing.

It was very, very cold when the Pilgrims landed. They were not used to such cold winters. Many of them were still tired and sick from the long ocean voyage. It was too late in the year to plant crops, so they had little food. More than half the Pilgrims died that first winter. At one time there were only six or seven persons who were well. These six or seven people had to take care of the sick, and they had to bury the dead. John Carver, the governor, died during that first winter. William Bradford was elected to take his place. Bradford was governor of the colony for 31 years.

The First Thanksgiving. In the spring an Indian came walking into the settlement. The Pilgrims were amazed when he said, "Welcome!" He had learned a little English from fishermen who had visited Maine. His name was Samoset.

Later, Samoset brought another Indian named Squanto. Squanto could speak more English than Samoset could. Squanto taught the Pilgrims how to plant corn. He told them the best places to go fishing and hunting.

One day Squanto came to Plymouth with a great chief named Massasoit. Massasoit made a treaty with the Pilgrims. In this treaty the Pilgrims and Indians said they would be friends. The Indians and the Pilgrims lived in peace for many years after that.

At the end of the first summer the Pilgrims had many things to be thankful for. They now had houses to protect them from the weather. They had raised enough corn to last them through the winter. They were at peace with the Indians. The Pilgrims knew that everything they had they owed to God. They decided to have a thanksgiving celebration.

Massasoit came with ninety Indians. They brought seven deer which they had shot in the forest. The Pilgrims supplied wild turkeys, corn, and pumpkins. The Pilgrims prayed and thanked God for helping them. Then they sat down with the Indians to a great feast. This was the first Thanksgiving. Today we celebrate Thanksgiving on the fourth Thursday of every November.

The Puritans Come to America.

Another group of English Protestants were called Puritans. Like the Pilgrims, they wished to come to America to worship God in their own way. The Puritans formed the Massachusetts Bay Company.

In 1628 the Massachusetts Bay Company sent a small group of settlers to North America. They started the village of Salem.

In 1630 about 1000 people from England came to the Massachusetts Bay Colony. They brought cattle, horses, seed, and tools. These people built their settlement at the mouth of the Charles River. The settlement later became known as Boston. John Winthrop was the leader of the Puritans who founded Boston. He became the first governor of the Colony.

The Pilgrims got along well. They sent fish, furs, and lumber to England. In a few years they had paid back the money which they had borrowed from the merchants.

More people came to the colony. By 1643 there were 3,000 settlers in Plymouth.

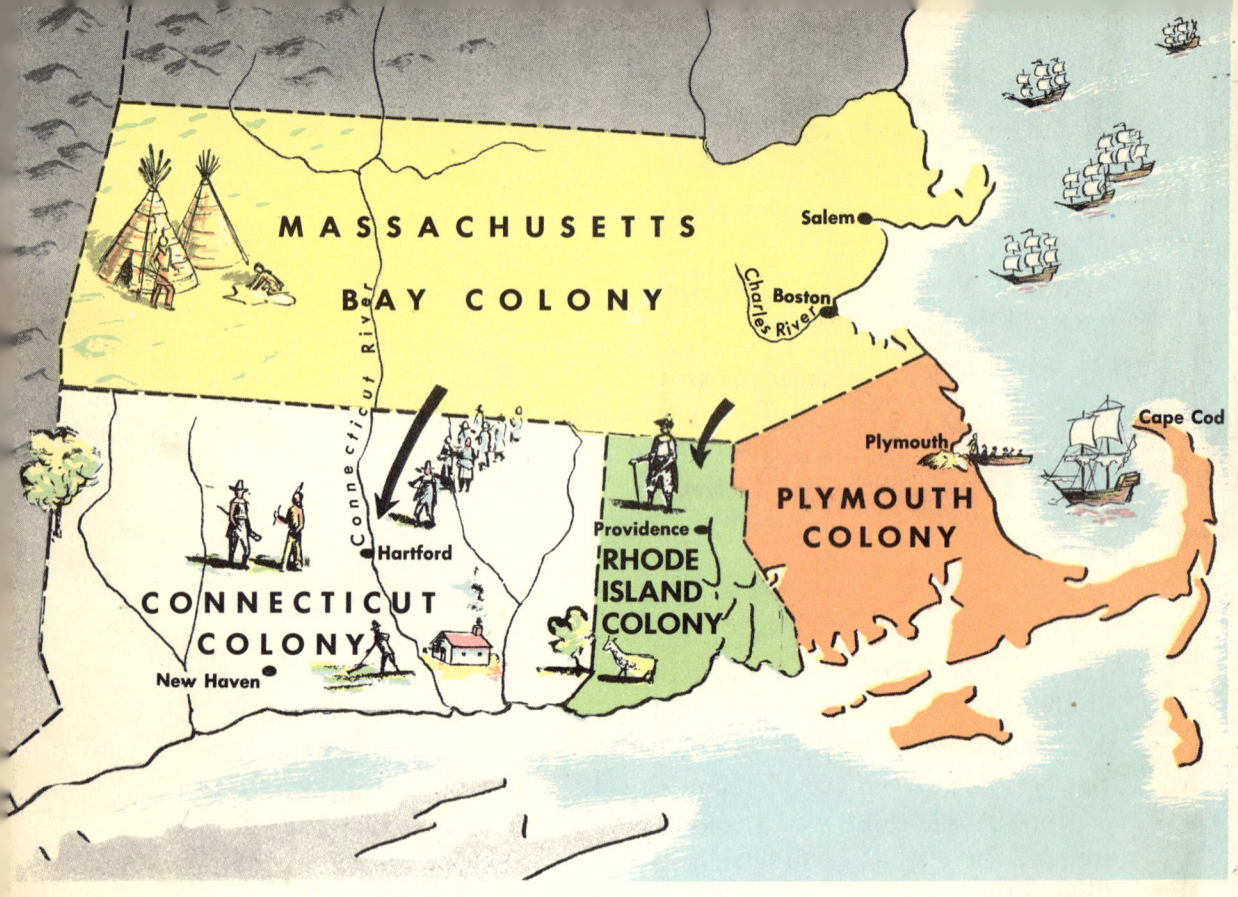

Between 1630 and 1640 many ships came to the Massachusetts Bay Colony. It grew faster than the near-by Plymouth Colony. By 1640 there were about 26,000 people in the colony. They had built many villages along the coast.

The Puritans left England because they did not want to be forced to belong to the Church of England. But in Massachusetts, they forced other people to accept their religion. Everyone was supposed to go to the Puritan Church whether he was a Puritan or not. Everyone was forced to give money to the Puritan Church.

Only Puritans were allowed to vote or to hold office. People who were not Puritans found that life was not very pleasant in the Massachusetts Bay Colony.

In 1690 the King of England ordered that Plymouth Colony and the Massachusetts Bay Colony should be combined into one colony. The new larger colony was called Massachusetts.

Roger Williams Founds Rhode Island. Roger Williams was a minister in Salem. He said some things that the Puritan leaders did not like.

He said that the Puritans had no right to force everyone to go to their church.

Roger Williams also said the land in North America belonged to the Indians. He said that the Puritans had no right to live in Massachusetts Bay Colony, unless the Indians gave them permission.

The Puritan leaders said that nobody would be allowed to say such things in their colony. They said that Roger Williams must go back to England. They sent soldiers to arrest him.

Roger Williams escaped into the forest before the soldiers could catch him. It was the middle of winter. The snow was deep and the weather was bitterly cold. Roger Williams pushed on. He reached the camp of his Indian friend, Chief Massasoit. By this time Williams was very sick. The Indians took care of him until he got better.

In the spring, Roger Williams started out on his travels once more. He found a place he thought would be good for a settlement. He bought the land from the Indians.

Roger Williams started a settlement which he called Providence. He said that in his settlement people would be allowed to go to whatever church they believed in. Many people from the other colonies moved to Providence.

In time, the settlement of Providence grew into the colony of Rhode Island.

Hooker Settles Connecticut. Thomas Hooker was an important minister in Massachusetts. Like Roger Williams, he did not agree with some of the ideas of the Puritan leaders. He thought everybody should have a voice in the government. The Puritan leaders wanted to control the government of Massachusetts. Thomas Hooker and most of the members of his parish decided to leave Massachusetts.

About a hundred people started out for the Connecticut River. They took their cattle with them. They traveled about seven or eight miles each day. Then they camped for the night.

On the banks of the Connecticut River, Hooker and his followers decided to settle. They bought land from the Indians and cleared it. They built homes, laid out farms and started a village which they called Hartford. Soon, several other villages grew up close by. These became the colony of Connecticut.

The people of Connecticut wanted a good government. They drew up a set of rules for their colony in 1639. These rules were called the Fundamental Orders of Connecticut. The rules gave the people a voice in their government. This was the first written constitution in our history.

What We Mean by New England. People who came to the New World from Europe did not want to forget the countries in which they had been born. The Spaniards gave the name New Spain to their land in the New World. The French gave the name New France to the land along the St. Lawrence River. We know that there was also a New Netherland and a New Sweden. In the same way, the English who settled in the northern part of our country called their land New England.

By the year 1700 there were four New England colonies. We have read that the colony of Massachusetts was formed by combining Plymouth Colony and the Massachusetts Bay Colony. We know that Rhode Island and Connecticut were started by settlers from Massachusetts.

The fourth New England colony was New Hampshire. It was also started by people from Massachusetts. New Hampshire was part of Massachusetts for many years. It became a separate colony in 1679.

PAUL, AN ENGLISH COLONIST

Paul lives in Massachusetts. His parents came from England. Paul belongs to the Puritan Church. There are many Puritans in Massachusetts. In other colonies there are many people belonging to other Protestant churches. There are very few Catholics in the English colonies. The few who are here live mostly in Maryland and Pennsylvania.

Paul owns his house and farm. He can do whatever he wishes with his farm. He votes for members of the assembly. The assembly decides important questions for the colony, for example, what taxes Paul must pay.

It would be wrong, however, to think that the English colonists were completely free. It was dangerous for a man to criticize the king or his officers. Negro slaves and certain kinds of servants had no freedom at all.

We see, then, that the English colonists had more freedom than the other colonists. They also had more freedom than most of the people of Europe. But they did not have as much freedom as we Americans have today.

NEW ENGLAND STATES

Today there are six New England states. Why are there six states where there were only four colonies?

The answer is that Maine and Vermont were never separate colonies. Maine was part of the colony of Massachusetts. Vermont was claimed by the colonies of New York and New Hampshire. After the colonies won their freedom from Great Britain, Maine and Vermont became separate states. That is how four colonies became six states.

STUDY LESSON

WHERE AM I? Answer each question in a complete sentence.

1. Which ocean did the Pilgrims cross to reach America?
2. Name the four New England colonies. Now name six states which came from those four New England colonies.
3. Which New England colonies became states after they won their freedom from Great Britain?
4. What large New England city was founded by the Puritans?

WHAT AM I? Write each word or name and after it the phrase that explains it.

1. Mayflower
2. settlement
3. Church of England
4. Mayflower Compact
5. The One True Church
6. Puritans

a. an agreement signed by the Pilgrims.
b. the Catholic Church.
c. people had to belong to it by law.
d. the ship that carried the Pilgrims to America.
e. a group of Protestants who did not belong to the Church of England.
f. a place where colonists made their new homes.

WHO AM I? Write each name and after it the phrase that tells about him.

1. Massasoit
2. Roger Williams
3. Thomas Hooker
4. William Bradford
5. Squanto
6. John Winthrop

a. founded the colony of Connecticut.
b. governor of Plymouth Colony.
c. first governor of the Massachusetts Bay Colony.
d. taught the Pilgrims how to plant corn.
e. Indian chief who made a treaty with the Pilgrims.
f. started Providence settlement.

WORDS TO KNOW. Use each of these words in a sentence. Look them up in your dictionary, if you are not sure of their meaning.

harbor   governor   agreement
colony   treaty   merchants

SOMETHING TO THINK ABOUT. Think carefully before you answer these questions.

1. Why do you think the founders of the United States made it a law that the government could not force us to go to church?
2. Do you think it would be a good thing if we had a law that all Americans must go to the Catholic Church?
3. Did the Puritans want to allow everyone to go to whatever church he pleased?

WHAT IS THE REASON? Think carefully before you answer each question.

1. Why did the Pilgrims and the Puritans leave England?
2. Why were the Pilgrims unhappy in Holland?
3. Why did the Pilgrims hold the first Thanksgiving?
4. Why did Roger Williams leave the Massachusetts Bay Colony?
5. Why did Plymouth Colony almost fail?

13. People From Many Countries Come to the

New Netherland Becomes New York. The man who is tearing up the note in the picture above is Peter Stuyvesant. He is the governor of New Netherland. It is the year 1664.

We read about New Netherland and Peter Stuyvesant in Chapter 11. You remember that New Netherland was the Dutch colony in North America. Peter Stuyvesant was the fourth governor of this colony.

The English had colonies both north and south of New Netherland. The English did not like to have a Dutch colony separating their colonies. The Dutch also had the best harbor along the coast, and the English did not like this.

The English leaders said, "The Dutch have no right to have a colony there. John Cabot claimed all of North America for England."

In the year 1664, three English warships sailed into the harbor of New Amsterdam. The English sent Peter Stuyvesant a note. They asked him to surrender.

In the picture we see Peter Stuyvesant tearing up the note. "I shall never surrender," he said.

The other picture shows what happened next.

When Peter Stuyvesant left, some of the Dutch settlers picked up the pieces of the note. They put the pieces together. They read the note.

"The English say that if we surrender without fighting we shall be allowed to keep our land," said one

Middle Colonies

of these Dutch settlers.

"Peter Stuyvesant is a very stern governor," said another settler.

"The people in the English colonies have more freedom than we do," said a third settler.

The news spread through New Amsterdam. Very few of the people liked the rule of Peter Stuyvesant. They would not fight for him.

So Peter Stuyvesant was forced to surrender without firing a shot. New Netherland became an English colony.

The King of England gave the colony to his brother, the Duke of York. The name New Netherland was changed to New York. The town of New Amsterdam became the town of New York.

Life in New Netherland. At first there were no women in the Dutch colony. Only men came over to trade with the Indians for furs. In 1624 two families came to live in the colony. They decided to settle on Manhattan Island near Fort Amsterdam. Soon there were 270 men, women, and children in the village called New Amsterdam.

The settlers started to build homes and lay out gardens. Dutch people love flowers. No Dutch family could live very long without a pretty garden of waving tulips and other bright flowers. They also planted vegetables to eat.

At first the settlers may have been a little homesick. When they started to build homes they wanted them to look like the houses they had left back home in Holland. They built them close together with long, sloping red roofs. Outside the front door each house had a little platform with steps going up to it. This was called a stoop. These stoops were the very first front porches in America. In summer the Dutch-American families used to sit on their stoops and chat with their neighbors next door.

The front door of a Dutch house was divided in two parts, upper and lower. They opened the top part to let in fresh air. The bottom part

115

was left shut to keep out stray animals.

Unlike early New England houses the Dutch houses had two or three stories. They were made of colored brick. The bricks were yellow and blue and red and brown. They were laid in fancy patterns. Pots of gay flowers sat on the windowsills. The Dutch people were not Puritans. They liked their homes to look pretty.

Inside and out, the Dutch homes were brushed and scrubbed till they shone. The Dutch housewives were famous for cleanliness. The center of family life was the fireplace. The Dutch fireplaces were not plain and simple like the ones in New England. They were made pretty with blue and white tiles with pictures on them. These pictures often told stories from the Bible.

A child could sit by the fire and learn his Bible history by studying the pictures and asking Mother questions about what he saw. Shining pots and pans and kettles were hung around the fireplace.

The Dutch homes had carved chairs and big beds and cupboards with open shelves. Here the housewife showed off her treasures of fine china and glowing pewter and shining silver. Some beds were closed out of sight in the daytime—very modern. Big, colored chests held fluffy piles of fresh towels, linens, blankets, and quilts.

A FAMOUS GOVERNOR OF NEW YORK

In 1682 the Duke of York made Thomas Dongan the governor of New York. Thomas Dongan was a Catholic. In those days it was very unusual for a Catholic to hold office either in England or in the English colonies.

Governor Dongan called together the first assembly in New York. The members of this assembly were elected by the people. They made laws for New York. This was the first time that the people of New York were given a voice in their government.

The first assembly passed a bill called "A Charter of Liberties." The charter said people could go to any church they wished. People could not be punished because of their religion. The charter said that people should always be allowed to elect their own lawmakers. It said that taxes could be made only by lawmakers who were elected by the people.

Governor Dongan was happy with the charter. He signed it and sent it to the Duke of York, in England. The Duke of York signed it, but he did not return it to New York. Therefore, the charter never became law.

The charter was very important even though it did not become law. Later, England used many parts of the charter in ruling her other colonies. Many parts of the charter were used later in the Constitution of New York State and in the Constitution of the United States.

Governor Dongan started the first post office in New York. He built important roads and signed treaties of peace with the Indians.

Thomas Dongan was governor of New York for only five years, but he was one of the greatest governors of colonial days.

New Jersey Becomes a Colony. The Duke of York did not keep all the land that had been taken from the Dutch. He gave the land between the Hudson and Delaware rivers to two of his friends. One of these friends was Lord John Berkeley. The other was Sir George Carteret. Sir George had once been the governor of the Island of Jersey. Therefore, he named the colony New Jersey. Neither Berkeley nor Carteret themselves ever came to this country, but Carteret sent his nephew, Philip Carteret, as the first governor of the colony.

In 1664 thirty English settlers came to New Jersey. They laid out a town and called it Elizabethtown. Later it became the city of Elizabeth. Then a band of Puritans who were unhappy in Connecticut came to New Jersey and started a town on the Passaic River. This was to become the city of Newark.

For a number of years the colony was governed by William Penn and a few other Quakers who bought it. While under the Quakers New Jersey kept good faith with the Indians. The people had a voice in the government through their assemblies, and freedom of religion was given to everyone. However in 1702 the colony was taken over by the King of England.

Then Catholics could no longer practice their religion, according to the law. In spite of the law, Father Farmer, New Jersey's first missionary, and Father Schneider, who was also a doctor, traveled about bringing the Mass and the sacraments to Catholics in the colony.

William Penn and Pennsylvania. An Englishman named George Fox started a new religion in 1647. He called this new religion the Society of Friends. The Friends were usually called Quakers.

The Quakers had a hard time in England. They would not belong to the Church of England. They believed it was wrong to take off their hats even to kings or noblemen. They believed that all war was wrong, and they taught that it was wrong even to join the army. The men who ruled England did not like these ideas. George Fox and his followers were put in prison many times.

The English people were amazed when William Penn became a Quaker. William Penn's father was Admiral Penn, a famous naval officer. The Penn family was very wealthy. Even though he came from a wealthy and well-known family, William Penn was put into prison for his beliefs.

William Penn wished to start a colony where there would be freedom of religion. There the Quakers could live in peace. People who belonged to other religions would also be allowed to live there and worship God in their own ways.

The King owed Admiral Penn a large sum of money. After Admiral Penn died, the king owed this money to William. William Penn asked the king if he would give him some land in America instead of the money. The king was glad to do this. Penn suggested that this land be called Sylvania. This means "woodland." The king put the name Penn in front of this, in honor of his old friend, Admiral Penn. That is how the colony came to be called Pennsylvania.

Three thousand people came to Penn's colony in 1681. Penn himself came the next year. He laid out a city which he called Philadelphia. This means "City of Brotherly Love."

Penn made friends with the Indians. He and the Indians signed a treaty of peace. As long as Penn lived his settlers had no trouble with the Indians.

These were years of great trouble in Europe. There were many wars. In some countries people were suffering for their religion. Some people did not have work and did not have enough to eat. Many of these people were glad to get away from Europe. Many came to Pennsylvania. They were welcomed by William Penn.

Some people came to Pennsylvania from Germany. In their own country the Germans are called *Deutsch*. The English-speaking people did not pronounce this word correctly. They said "Dutch" instead of "Deutsch." That is why the Germans in Pennsylvania were called the "Pennsylvania Dutch," although they were not Dutch at all.

People also came to Pennsylvania from Scotland, Ireland, and many other places.

Many Catholics came to Pennsylvania. In most of the English colonies Catholics were not allowed to practice their religion, but in Pennsylvania they were. Penn tried to form a true Christian community. He wanted justice, freedom, and kindness to be the rule.

Large groups of German and Dutch settlers came to Pennsylvania in 1683. They settled at a place which they called Germantown

Delaware. We have already read that the Swedes settled at the mouth of the Delaware River. They called their colony New Sweden. Later, the Dutch captured New Sweden. Then the English took over all the land ruled by the Dutch. The land that had been New Sweden was then called Delaware.

The Swedes kept on living in Delaware although it was captured first by the Dutch and then by the English. Many other settlers later joined the Swedes.

William Penn was given Delaware because it was across the river from his colony. Delaware was given its own government in 1703.

which is now part of Philadelphia. These people were skilled weavers, silversmiths, lacemakers, and printers. Before 1690 they built the first paper mill in America.

What We Mean by the Middle Colonies. This map shows the four colonies that we read about in this chapter. They are called the Middle Colonies. Do you know why? The reason is that the four New England colonies were to the north of them and the five Southern Colonies were to the south of them. So the Middle Colonies were right in the middle between New England and the South.

In New England almost all the settlers were English. In the Middle Colonies most of the settlers were English, but there were also many settlers from other countries. There were Swedes in Delaware. There were Dutch in New York. There were Germans, Scotch, Irish, and people from many other countries in Pennsylvania. All these people were ruled by English laws. In time, everyone learned to speak English.

STUDY LESSON

WHERE IS IT? Answer each question in a complete sentence.

1. Which state did the Dutch colony of New Netherland become?
2. Which waterway did the Dutch use when they traveled north in their New Netherland colony?
3. What two rivers formed the boundaries of the New Jersey colony?
4. Which city was founded by William Penn?
5. Can you name the Middle Colonies?

WHAT AM I? Write each name and after it the phrase that explains it.

1. New Amsterdam
2. New Sweden
3. Pennsylvania Dutch
4. Quakers
5. Pennsylvania

a. named in honor of Admiral Penn.
b. taught that it was wrong to go to war.
c. later became New York City.
d. came from Germany.
e. later became Delaware.

SOMETHING TO THINK ABOUT. Think carefully before you answer these questions.

1. Do you think Peter Stuyvesant was a good governor?
2. What reasons did the Dutch have for surrendering New Netherland without firing a shot?

WHO AM I? Write each name and after it the phrase that tells about him.

1. Peter Stuyvesant   2. John Cabot
3. Duke of York   4. George Fox
5. Admiral Penn

a. claimed all of North America for England.
b. started the Quaker religion.
c. brother of the King of England.
d. Governor of New Netherland.
e. was given land in America for money owed to him.

WHAT IS THE REASON? Think carefully before you answer each question.

1. Why did the English want the Dutch colony of New Amsterdam?
2. Why did the Quakers leave England to come to Pennsylvania?
3. Why did many Catholics come to Pennsylvania rather than to some of the other English colonies?
4. Why were New York, New Jersey, Pennsylvania, and Delaware called the Middle Colonies?

WORDS TO KNOW. Use each of these words in a sentence. Look them up in your dictionary if you are not sure of their meaning.

surrender   noblemen   freedom
coast   laws   society

14. The Southern Colonies

Virginia, First Southern Colony. We have learned how the New England Colonies were founded. Then we found out how the Middle Colonies were started. In this chapter we will read about the Southern Colonies. We have already read about Virginia, the first Southern colony.

We know that the first English settlement in North America was at Jamestown. The colony of Virginia grew from this settlement. For a time, Virginia was the only English colony in North America. Even after the Pilgrims and Puritans settled in New England, there were no colonies close to Virginia.

Then some neighbors moved in near Virginia. The first neighbor was Maryland. This is north of Virginia, as you can see on the map on the next page.

Catholics Come to Maryland. Many of the settlers in this picture are Catholics. They have just arrived on the coast of North America. They have brought two priests with them. One of the priests is saying Mass. He is Father Andrew White. It is March 25, 1634.

Behind the settlers you can see two ships. They are the *Ark* and the *Dove*. These two ships have brought the settlers from England to North America.

The Catholic settlers are happy to be in a place where they can attend Mass. Back in England, people who attended Mass were fined or put into prison. Priests who were caught saying Mass could be put to death.

How did these settlers happen to come to America? This is the way it happened:

The first Lord Baltimore was an important man in England. He became a Catholic. He felt sorry for his fellow Catholics. He asked the king if he could start a colony where Catholics would be allowed to practice their religion. The king gave Lord Baltimore a large piece of land north of Virginia. The king said the colony should be called Maryland.

The first Lord Baltimore died before he could start the colony of Maryland. His son, the second Lord Baltimore, decided to carry out his father's plans. He could not come to America, so he sent his brother, Leonard Calvert, to be the governor. Leonard Calvert crossed the ocean with the first settlers. We can see him in the picture above. He and the second priest are kneeling in front of the other settlers.

Religious Freedom in Maryland. Not all settlers who came to live in Maryland were Catholics. Many of them were Protestants. Leonard Calvert said that the Protestants would be allowed to practice their religion. He said there would be freedom of religion in Maryland. Maryland was the first of the English colonies to grant freedom of religion.

You probably remember that Roger Williams said there would be freedom of religion in Rhode Island. Maryland was founded two years before Rhode Island.

At first, everything went well for the settlers. The Indians were friendly. Governor Calvert paid the Indians for the land the settlers were using. An Indian chief gave Father White his own hut to use as a chapel. The Indian braves helped the white men clear the land and build houses. The squaws taught the women how to make bread out

of Indian corn. Like their neighbors in Virginia, the settlers raised tobacco and sent it to England.

In 1649 the people of Maryland passed a new law. This law was called the Toleration Act. It said that every Christian would have freedom of religion. This was a good law, but there was freedom of religion in Maryland even before the law was passed.

Some years later the king said that Maryland would no longer belong to Lord Baltimore. The king said that now Maryland would have to be ruled by the same laws as England. This meant that the Toleration Act would no longer be in effect. After that, the Catholics had much to suffer in the colony that had been started for them.

The Carolinas. South of Virginia the land was very fertile. It was well suited for growing tobacco and rice. Planters from Virginia started to move to this area.

In 1587 Sir Walter Raleigh had sent a party which settled in what later became North Carolina. The settlement did not last, but here the first English child was born in America in 1587. Her name was Virginia Dare.

In 1663 the king gave the land south of Virginia to eight of his friends. This new colony was called Carolina. Later, it was divided into two parts: North Carolina and South Carolina. Settlers built towns at Albemarle and Charles Town.

The first settlement that lasted in South Carolina was made in 1670 and called Charles Town in honor of the king. Trade with the Indians and shipping furs to England made the colony prosper.

Georgia Is Founded in 1733. There were some very strict laws in England. A man who could not pay the money he owed was sent to prison. Sometimes, his whole family were sent to prison with him. The prisons were horrible places. They were cold in the winter and hot in the summer. They were dirty. They had little fresh air. Many of the prisoners took sick and died.

A man named James Oglethorpe visited some of the prisons. He was shocked by what he saw.

"Why punish these people?" he asked. "They have done nothing wrong. It is not their fault if they have no money. This way they will never be able to pay what they owe. They cannot earn money while they are in prison."

James Oglethorpe asked King George for some land in America. He wanted to start a colony for the people who owed debts. There, the people would be able to lead useful lives. This would be much better than keeping them in prison.

King George did not have much land left. But there was a little between South Carolina and Florida. This land was claimed by both England and Spain. King George was afraid some Spaniards from Florida might move into this land. He was glad to give it to James Oglethorpe. In this way, there would be Englishmen instead of Spaniards living on the land.

Oglethorpe started his new colony in 1733. He named it Georgia, in honor of King George II, who was the King of England.

Georgia was the thirteenth, and last, English colony. It was settled 126 years after the first English settlers came to Jamestown. George Washington was already one year old when Georgia was founded. James Oglethorpe lived to see Georgia become a state instead of a colony. It was one of the thirteen original states.

We have now read how all the English colonies were founded. There were thirteen of these colonies. Four were New England Colonies. Four were Middle Colonies. Five were Southern Colonies.

On the map above you see all thirteen of the colonies. In the next chapter we shall read how the people lived in these colonies.

128

STUDY LESSON

WHERE IS IT? Answer each question in a complete sentence.

1. Maryland was north of what colony?
2. Which colony was just south of Virginia?
3. Name the Southern colonies.
4. Which English colony was located between South Carolina and Florida?

WHAT AM I? Write each name and after it the phrase that explains it.

1. Maryland
2. Jamestown
3. Georgia
4. Toleration Act
5. Florida
6. Carolina

a. a law that gave Maryland's colonists freedom of religion.
b. a Spanish colony.
c. the first English settlement in North America.
d. first colony to grant freedom of religion.
e. colony started for people in debt.
f. land south of Virginia.

WHAT IS THE REASON? Think carefully before you answer each question.

1. Why was Maryland colony started?
2. Why did Oglethorpe found the colony of Georgia?
3. Why did Catholics have to suffer in Maryland in later years?
4. Why did King George allow Oglethorpe to start a colony in Georgia?

WORDS TO KNOW. Use each of these words in a sentence. Look them up in your dictionary if you are not sure of their meaning.

| tobacco | debts | neighbors |
| chapel | | prison |

WHO AM I? Write each name and after it the phrase that tells about him.

1. Lord Baltimore
2. James Oglethorpe
3. Leonard Calvert
4. Father Andrew White
5. George II

a. the King of England.
b. used an Indian hut as a chapel.
c. was given land by King George.
d. brother of Lord Baltimore.
e. became a Catholic in England.

SOMETHING TO THINK ABOUT. Think carefully before you answer these questions.

1. How did Maryland show that Catholics believe in freedom of religion?
2. Do you think that it was a good idea to put people in prison because they owed money?
3. What other reason, besides kindness to debtors, did the King have for allowing James Oglethorpe to start a colony in Georgia?

15. How People Lived in the English Colonies

Living in the Middle Colonies. Farming and trading were the chief occupations. Farmers raised wheat, corn, oats, and rye. Fruit trees did well and there were good grazing lands for cows and sheep. Milk, cheese and butter, and wool and yarn were leading products.

New York and Philadelphia were both good ports, so ship owners and traders got rich. Ships carried goods back and forth from New England and the South to the Middle Colonies. Fur trade with the Indians was most profitable because the Indians traded their expensive furs for cheap beads and liquor.

You have already seen how the Dutch people lived in their part of the Middle Colonies. Now you are going to see how English settlers lived close by in another part of the Middle Colonies.

A Family in Pennsylvania. This is the Taylor family. The Taylors live on a farm in Pennsylvania. It is the year 1720.

The Taylors are all in the kitchen. The kitchen was the most important room in a colonial house. The mother cooked the meals over the big open fireplace, as you see in the picture on page 133. In cold weather the kitchen was the only warm room in the house. Everybody stayed near the fireplace and did their work near the fireplace. They ate in the kitchen. Sometimes some members of the family even slept in the kitchen.

Mr. Taylor came to America from England twenty years ago, in 1700. He was a Catholic, so he settled in Pennsylvania. At that time Pennsylvania was the only English colony in which Catholics were allowed to practice their religion.

Mr. Taylor's land was covered by trees when he first saw it. He had to cut down many trees in order to make room for a house. Men from other farms helped him build his house. Then he had to cut down more trees so he could plant his crops. All this was very hard work. Mr. Taylor married after living in Pennsylvania for several years.

All the Taylor children were born on the farm in Pennsylvania. They have never been more than 20 miles from the farm. The roads are very bad, and it is not easy to travel. They have never seen a city. Sometimes, in the evenings when the work is done, Mr. Taylor tells them about the big ocean he crossed when he came to America. It is hard for the children to picture such things.

"But you should thank God that you are here in Pennsylvania," Mr. Taylor says. "When I was in England I was not allowed to practice my religion. I could not find any work to do. I was often cold and hungry. Once when I could not pay a small sum of money that I owed I was put into prison.

"Here it is different. Here, a priest comes around every month to say Mass for us. Catholics meet once a week to say prayers together.

We own this large farm. We do have to work hard, but we have a house, we have plenty of food, and we have warm clothes. Back where I come from we would not have any of these things."

Everybody Worked on a Colonial Farm. Take another look at the picture at the beginning of this chapter. You will notice that everybody is working. Men, women, and children all worked on a colonial farm. They worked from early in the morning till late at night.

The Taylors do almost everything for themselves. They raise all their own food. They make all their own clothes. They make their own furniture. They even make the candles which they need for lights. The only things they buy are their tools.

Do the Taylor children go to

school? The boys attend school a few months in the winter. There is not so much work to do on the farm in the winter. They learn to read and write and they learn something about numbers. They do not learn much else. The girls do not go to school at all. Their mother teaches them how to cook and sew.

Mr. and Mrs. Taylor both teach the children the truths of their Catholic faith.

Do the Taylors ever have any good times? Yes, but their good times are different from yours. They have no movies, no radio, no television. They make their own good times. The girls have homemade dolls. The boys have homemade sleds. Sometimes the neighbors gather together. They sing songs, dance, and play games.

How People in New England Lived. We have just had a look at the Taylor family. The Taylors lived in Pennsylvania. Suppose the Taylors had lived in one of the other colonies instead of Pennsylvania. Suppose they had lived in one of the New England colonies, for example.

If the Taylors had lived in New England their lives would have been the same in some ways. In other ways their lives would have been different.

If they had lived in New England they probably would have been farmers just as they were in Pennsylvania. Nine out of ten people in all the English colonies were farmers.

In New England the farms were smaller than in Pennsylvania. The ground was not as good for raising crops and there were many stones. This meant that New England farmers had to work very hard to make a living.

Many of the people in New England lived in villages. They went out from the village every day to work in the fields. The houses in a village were often built around an open space. This space was called the village green. Anyone might bring his cows to feed on the grass of the green. The men of the village sometimes drilled here, like soldiers. Boys sometimes played marbles on the green.

Every village had a blacksmith. His chief task was to make iron shoes for the horses. He also made iron pots and kettles and many kinds of tools.

Each village also had a carpenter and a cobbler. A cobbler is a man who makes shoes.

The House. The house was long and narrow. The door opened on a tiny hall with the living room on one side and the family bedroom on the other. There might be a

No Freedom of Religion in New England. The Taylors could hear Mass. If they had lived in New England they probably would not have been able to hear Mass. Priests were not allowed in most of the New England colonies.

There was a Puritan Church in almost every village. The people had to go to this church or else pay a fine. For this reason, not many Catholics went to New England.

The New England colonies had more schools than the other colonies. Everyone had to pay a tax to support the schools, just as our public schools are supported today. The Puritan religion was taught in these schools, along with reading, writing, and arithmetic.

The people of New England did not have half as much fun as the people of other colonies. The Puritans did not allow card playing, dancing, and many other kinds of amusements. They thought these things were sinful.

small bedroom upstairs. There was no kitchen.

The huge living room served for cooking and eating and working. A big fireplace gave heat and light. Mother cooked in kettles hung over the fire. She baked in a brick oven on one side. Grown-ups sat before the fire on a long, plain bench with a high back to keep out drafts. Children sat on three-legged stools in the chimney corner. Almost every living room had a spinning wheel for making thread, a loom for making cloth, and a churn for making butter.

The People of New England Turn to the Sea. If the Taylors had lived in New England their father might not have been a farmer. He might have been a sailor or a fisherman, a lumberman or a rum trader.

Because the land was so poor, all the people of New England could not make their living by farming. There were many big trees in the forest. Some men became lumbermen. They cut down the trees and sawed them into boards. Some of the lumber was used in New England. Some of it was sent to Europe. Some New England men became shipbuilders. Some who lived near the ocean became sailors and fishermen.

Many of the richest people of New England made their money by trading with the islands in the West Indies. New England ships sailed to the Dutch and Spanish islands with cargoes of fish, lumber, flour, and wheat. The traders sold their goods and bought sugar and molasses. New Englanders used the molasses to make rum, a favorite drink in the colonies.

Some of the rum was shipped from New England to Africa and exchanged for slaves. The slaves were brought to the West Indies and exchanged for more molasses. The molasses was then brought to New England to make more rum.

The New Englanders made money on each sale. The rum makers, ship owners, and slave traders were getting rich. Later on when England tried to stop this trade, these wealthy shippers were ready to rebel. This was one of the causes of the American Revolution.

How the Colonies Were Governed. John Adams belongs to the Massachusetts Colony. We ask him how the colony is governed. He tells us that the assembly makes most of the laws.

"There is also a Parliament in England," John says. "This Parliament makes laws for England and all the lands ruled by England. So we have to obey Parliament as well as our assembly. Parliament can also set aside laws which were passed by our assembly. It has not done this very often. I am afraid there would be trouble if Parliament set aside many laws passed by our assembly. I hope that will never happen."

John also tells us that Massachusetts has a governor who is appointed by the King of England. This governor does not have as much power as the governor of New France or the viceroy of New Spain.

"The assembly pays the governor's salary," John tells us. "And we elect the members of the assembly. If the governor does something we do not like we can stop paying his salary. No governor wants this to happen."

We ask John if the government is the same in each of the thirteen English colonies.

"There are small differences," he says. "But in most ways the governments are alike. Each colony has a governor and each colony has an assembly. And, of course, each colony is under the Parliament in England."

We ask John if all the people of Massachusetts have the right to vote.

"No," he says. "Women are not allowed to vote. Nor are all the men. Usually only men who own a certain amount of property are allowed to vote in any of the English colonies except Pennsylvania.

We can see that even the people in the English colonies did not have complete self-government. This was because so few people were allowed to vote. But the colonists were very proud of what self-government they did have. The people in the French and Spanish lands had no self-government at all.

Later American colonists thought England was trying to take away their self-government. This frightened them very much. The American colonists always loved their freedom. We shall see how the fear of losing their freedom made the colonists break away from England. This is how our country, the United States of America, began.

How People Lived in the Southern Colonies. In the Southern Colonies there were large farms which were called plantations. Usually, one large crop was raised on each plantation. Tobacco was raised on some plantations. Rice was raised on others. Indigo was raised on others. Indigo is a plant from which blue dye can be made.

Tobacco, rice, and indigo were not grown to be used by the planters. They were raised to be sold. Such crops are called staple crops or money crops. Tobacco was the money crop grown in the South for many, many years. Later cotton became the money crop. These money crops made the owners of the plantation or planters wealthy.

Most of the plantations were near a river. Each plantation had a wharf. Ocean vessels came up to the wharfs. The ships sailed off to England loaded with tobacco, or rice, or indigo. They came back with clothes, books, and furniture which the plantation owners had ordered from England. The plantation owners never lost touch with England. They did not have to make everything for themselves as did the Taylors and most other farmers of New England and the Middle Colonies.

hospitality. The friendly welcome shown to guests is called hospitality.

Travel from plantation to plantation was not easy. Many of the plantations were located on rivers. These could be reached by boats—a common means of transportation in those days. Many years later roads were made. Then travel by horse and carriage became possible. Horse-drawn carriages which traveled over a regular route were called stagecoaches. The distance between two stops on a trip was called a stage.

The planters needed a great deal of help. Negro slaves did most of the work on the plantations. These slaves belonged to the plantation owners. They were not paid for their work. They were given a place to live, and food, and clothes, but that was about all. They were not allowed to run away. Slaves were bought and sold like animals.

The wealthy Southern planters could afford to build beautiful homes. These houses were made of brick, stone, and timber. The woodwork inside was of the finest woods often brought from Europe. Outside, the houses were decorated with broad columns and usually painted white.

These houses had many rooms for the family and their guests. Since the plantations were so large, the only neighbors were far, far away. Visiting became the custom. Southern families took great pride in making their guests feel at home. Southerners became known for their

COTTON PLANTATION

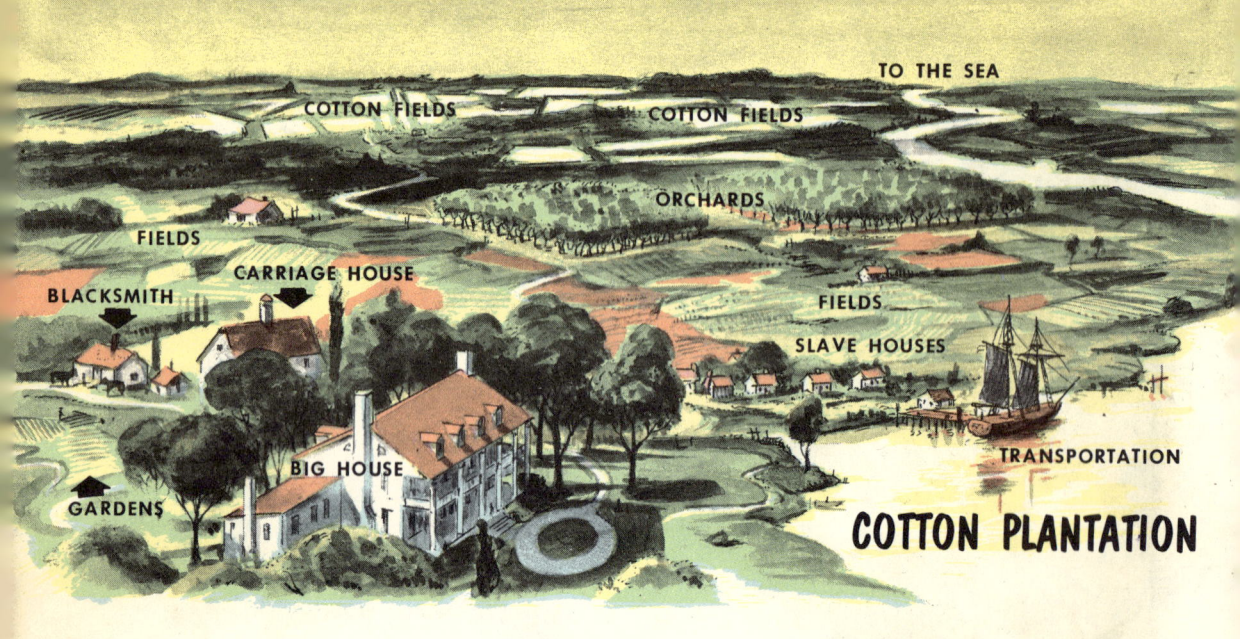

Every plantation had its own garden patch. Here corn, wheat, and vegetables such as potatoes, carrots, turnips, and parsnips were grown. Pear trees and apple trees provided fresh fruit. These crops were not for sale. They were for the planter and his family and slaves to eat.

Each plantation had its own carpenters and blacksmiths. There were few schools in the South. Many plantation owners hired teachers, or tutors, for the children. Some of the boys were sent to England to go to school.

Not all the farmers of the South lived on large plantations. Far back from the rivers and the ocean were many small farms. The people who lived on these farms did not have any slaves. They had to work very hard for a living.

Most of the children who lived on these small farms did not go to school. The children of the slaves did not go to school either.

The Southern plantation owners had many ways of having a good time. They loved horse racing and hunting, dancing and card playing.

If the Taylors had lived in the Southern Colonies they would not have been allowed to practice their religion. Everyone had to belong to the Church of England in these colonies. Maryland, as we know, was started for the Catholics. But even in Maryland, after 1689, Catholics were punished for practicing their religion.

STUDY LESSON

WHERE IS IT? Answer each question in a complete sentence.

1. Name the English colonies.
2. Along what coast of America are the English colonies?
3. Is Pennsylvania a New England, a Middle, or a Southern colony?
4. In what colonies were plantations found?
5. In what colonies was farming most difficult?

WHAT AM I? Write each word and after it the phrase that explains it.

   1. plantation 2. cobbler 3. village
   4. indigo   5. slaves   6. tobacco

a. a man who makes shoes
b. a plant from which blue dye is made.
c. a crop raised on Southern plantations.
d. a very large farm in the Southern colonies.
e. a place where houses are built close together.
f. Negroes who worked on large Southern plantations.

WORDS TO KNOW. Use each of these words in a sentence. Look them up in your dictionary if you are not sure of their meaning.

   plow   dye   wharf
   tax   tutors   mansion

WHAT IS THE REASON? Think carefully before you answer each question.

1. Why did Mr. Taylor come to Pennsylvania instead of coming to one of the other English colonies?
2. Why was the Taylor family better off on a farm in Pennsylvania than they would have been in Europe?
3. Why did New England farmers have to work very hard to make a living?
4. Why did plantation owners in the Southern Colonies have slaves?
5. Why did the people of other colonies have better times than the people from New England?

SOMETHING TO THINK ABOUT. Think carefully before you answer these questions.

1. Are Catholics now allowed to practice their religion everywhere in the United States? Do you know if they are allowed to practice their religion everywhere in the world today?
2. Why should Catholics love their country?
3. Imagine! In Pennsylvania there were so few priests that Mass could be heard only once a month. How many times a day is Mass said in your parish?

GAMES   ART

SCRAPBOOK OF FAMOUS PEOPLE

ADD THESE STORIES TO YOUR SCRAPBOOK WITH PICTURES OR DRAWINGS OF THE MEN.

PETER STUYVESANT FORCED THE SETTLERS TO BELONG TO THE DUTCH REFORMED CHURCH AND REFUSED TO LET THE SETTLERS HAVE A VOICE IN THE GOVERNMENT. IF YOU WERE A DUTCH SETTLER WOULD YOU HAVE FOUGHT FOR STUYVESANT OR SURRENDERED TO THE ENGLISH? WRITE A LITTLE STORY ABOUT THE DUTCH GOVERNOR.

IF THE KING OWED YOU SOME MONEY WOULD YOU HAVE TAKEN INSTEAD A PIECE OF LAND IN THE WILDERNESS WHERE PEOPLE COULD PRACTICE THEIR OWN RELIGION? **WILLIAM PENN** DID. WRITE A STORY TELLING ABOUT PENN.

JAMES OGLETHORPE FELT SORRY FOR THE PEOPLE HE SAW BEING KEPT IN PRISON BECAUSE THEY WERE TOO POOR TO PAY THEIR DEBTS. WRITE A STORY ABOUT HIM SHOWING THE KIND OF PERSON HE WAS.

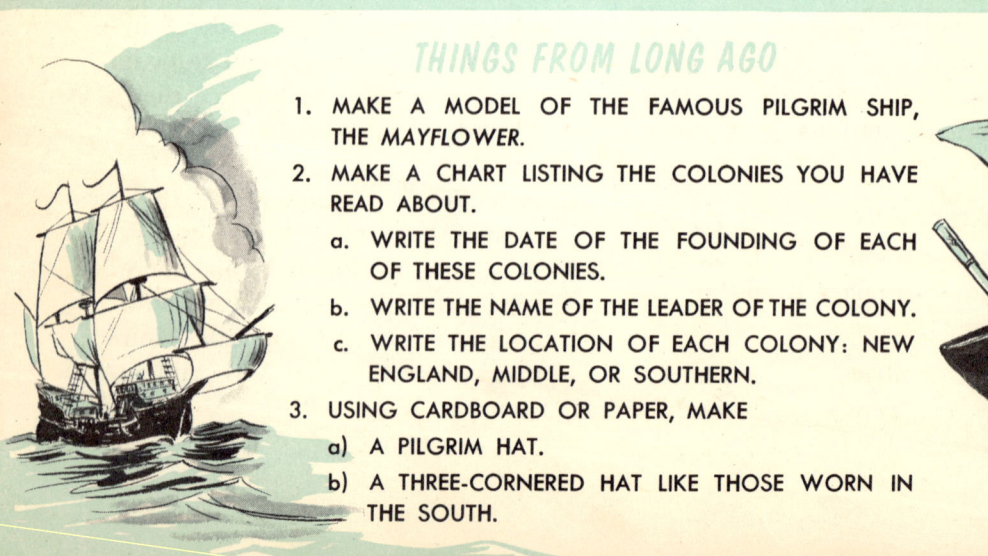

THINGS FROM LONG AGO

1. MAKE A MODEL OF THE FAMOUS PILGRIM SHIP, THE *MAYFLOWER*.
2. MAKE A CHART LISTING THE COLONIES YOU HAVE READ ABOUT.
    a. WRITE THE DATE OF THE FOUNDING OF EACH OF THESE COLONIES.
    b. WRITE THE NAME OF THE LEADER OF THE COLONY.
    c. WRITE THE LOCATION OF EACH COLONY: NEW ENGLAND, MIDDLE, OR SOUTHERN.
3. USING CARDBOARD OR PAPER, MAKE
    a) A PILGRIM HAT.
    b) A THREE-CORNERED HAT LIKE THOSE WORN IN THE SOUTH.

BOOKS   PLAYS

THIS IS HOW IT HAPPENED

PLAN A PLAY CALLED "QUIET CONQUEST"

SCENE I: PETER STUYVESANT GIVES ORDERS TO THE DUTCH SETTLERS.

SCENE II: PETER STUYVESANT RECEIVES THE NOTE FROM THE ENGLISH AND TEARS IT UP. THE DUTCH READ THE TORN NOTE AND TALK ABOUT SURRENDER.

SCENE III: THE ENGLISH ARRIVE AND TAKE COMMAND. THE PLACE IS NAMED NEW YORK.

SEEING AMERICA

DRAW OR TRACE A MAP OF THE ATLANTIC COAST OF NORTH AMERICA AND MARK THE LOCATION OF THE THIRTEEN COLONIES. COLOR THE NEW ENGLAND COLONIES GREEN, THE MIDDLE COLONIES RED, AND THE SOUTHERN COLONIES BLUE.

NAME GAME

USING THE NAMES OF PERSONS WHO HAVE APPEARED IN UNIT THREE, PLAY THE GAME WHICH WAS DESCRIBED AT THE END OF UNIT ONE.

COLONIAL INFORMATION CENTER

IF YOU HAD LIVED DURING COLONIAL TIMES, LIFE WOULD HAVE BEEN VERY DIFFERENT FOR YOU. WHAT GAMES WOULD YOU HAVE PLAYED? HOW WOULD YOU HAVE LIKED SCHOOL THEN? IN A LIBRARY YOU WILL FIND MANY BOOKS ON THE LIVES OF COLONIAL CHILDREN. HERE ARE A FEW YOU MIGHT LOOK FOR.

DE ANGELI	ELIN'S AMERIKA	DOUBLEDAY
	JARED'S ISLAND	DOUBLEDAY
	SKIPPACK SCHOOL	DOUBLEDAY
HUMPHREY	HOW NEW ENGLAND WAS MADE	LOTHROP, LEE & SHEPARD
MALOY AND DALGLIESH	WOODEN SHOES IN AMERICA	SCRIBNER
PERKINS	THE PURITAN TWINS	HOUGHTON MIFFLIN
	PILGRIM STORIES AND PLAYS	RAND McNALLY
STONE AND FICKETT	EVERYDAY LIFE IN THE COLONIES	HEATH

Unit Four

A NEW NATION

Looking Into the Long Ago

"Now, if you will turn off the lights," said Mr. North, "I will show the movies."

"I took these pictures at our Fourth of July picnic," Mr. North said, "but I have never seen them myself. I do not own a projector. When I heard the Davis family was coming, I borrowed a projector."

"I can hardly wait to see the pictures," said Mary Jean.

Mr. North clicked the switch on the projector. The screen lighted up. In a moment, the North and Davis families were watching their Fourth of July picnic.

"Oh look," Mary said. "Dick and I are playing 'last tag'. I didn't know you took pictures of that, Uncle Tom. Look! There I go over the brook. I am crossing on the stones. I made it! Now here comes Dick after me."

"Oh, oh," Dick groaned. He knew what was going to happen next.

The movies showed Dick stepping from stone to stone. When he got to the middle of the brook, his foot slipped. He went into the water with a splash.

Everyone in the room laughed at the picture of Dick sitting in the water.

Suddenly the picture on the screen changed. There was no longer a picture of Dick sitting in the water. Now there was a picture of a man's head.

"Who is that?" asked Dick.

"That's a man who lived a long time ago," said Mary Jean. "You can tell by his clothes and by the way he wears his hair."

"What is he doing in our Fourth of July pictures?" Dick asked.

Mr. North turned off the projector. Dick turned on the lights.

Mr. North was laughing when the lights came on.

"After the picnic I had a little film left in the camera," he said. "I wanted to use it up. I also wanted to see whether I could photograph a picture from a book. I found this picture of Thomas Jefferson in one of my books. It turned out well, didn't it?"

"Yes," Dick said, "but I do not like having Thomas Jefferson on our Fourth of July film."

"I can cut him off if you want me to," said Mr. North. "But you should not mind having Thomas Jefferson on a Fourth of July film. What is the Fourth of July?"

"It is our country's birthday."

"That is right. The people who lived in the English colonies did not like the way England was treating them. These people elected some men to a Congress. The members of Congress signed a Declaration of Independence. They adopted it on July 4, 1776."

Mr. North was now putting the projector back into the case.

"Do you know who wrote the Declaration of Independence?" he asked.

"I'll bet I can guess," said Mary Jean. "Was it Thomas Jefferson?"

"Yes," said Mr. North. "Some day you will learn part of the Declaration of Independence. You will learn the part which says that all men are created equal. You will learn the part which says that all men have certain rights which cannot be taken away. Those are important words, and you will understand them better when you are a little older. It was Thomas Jefferson who wrote those words."

"Well," said Dick, "I guess you will not have to cut Thomas Jefferson off the Fourth of July film. He really belongs there." Then Dick remembered the picture of himself falling into the brook. "In fact," he said, "I wish there were more of Jefferson and less of me."

16. The French Lose Their Land in North America

Washington Carries a Message. The young man in this picture is George Washington. He is 21 years old. It is the year 1753. The governor of Virginia has sent George Washington on a very important errand.

What is the errand? We shall understand it better if we look at the map.

The thirteen English colonies, as you see, were along the shores of the Atlantic Ocean. The people who lived in the colonies were called colonists. Very few of the colonists crossed the Appalachian Mountains at first. By 1750 some of the colonists were thinking about crossing the mountains. They wished to build homes and start farms near the Ohio River. You can see the Ohio River on the map.

The colonists were sure that the Ohio Valley belonged to them. John Cabot had claimed all of North America for the English.

But the French were also sure that the Ohio Valley belonged to them. La Salle had stood at the mouth of the Mississippi River and had claimed all the land drained by that river.

"The Ohio River empties into the Mississippi River," the French said. "Therefore, the Ohio country belongs to us."

The French began building forts in the Ohio country. They did this so they could keep soldiers there. The soldiers would keep the English settlers from moving into the rich Ohio country.

The governor of Virginia was angry when he learned what the French were doing. He wanted to tell them to stop building forts. Who could he send with the important message? He selected George Washington, who was then a major in the army.

That is why we see George Washington crossing the mountains in the winter of 1753. He is carrying an important message from the governor of Virginia to the commander of the French soldiers in the Ohio country.

The message says that the Ohio country belongs to the English. The message asks the French to stop building forts there.

FRENCH FORTS IN THE OHIO COUNTRY

How the French and Indian War Began. Major Washington delivered his message. The French general told Washington that the French would not leave the Ohio Valley.

Washington had a long, dangerous trip back to Virginia. Indians shot arrows at him and his men. He nearly lost his life when his raft turned over in an icy stream. He and his men had to sleep on the frozen ground with no tents over them. At last Washington reached Virginia. He told the governor that the French would not stop building forts.

In 1754 the governor sent Washington back to the Ohio country with some soldiers. Washington's small army was surrounded by French and Indians. Washington was forced to surrender, and so he returned to Virginia.

The French and Indian War had begun. The English called it the French and Indian War, because they had to fight both French soldiers and Indian warriors. Most of the Indians were on the side of the French. The Iroquois Indians, however, were on the side of the English. The Iroquois had been enemies of the French ever since the days of Champlain.

The King of England sent General Edward Braddock to take charge of the English Army in America. General Braddock decided to capture Fort Duquesne. The French had built this important fort at the place where two rivers join to form the Ohio River.

General Braddock had done much fighting in Europe. Most of this fighting was done on open fields. He did not know very much about fighting in the forests of North America. Braddock had his men march as if they were in a parade. Their flags waved in the breeze. The French and Indians shot at them from behind trees and stones. The British soldiers wore bright red coats. These made good targets for the French and Indians. Many of Braddock's men were killed. Braddock himself was wounded and later died from the wounds. After General Braddock was wounded, George Washington took charge of the army. He saved what was left of it.

The War Ends. For every Frenchman in North America there were about 18 English colonists. You would think that it would have been easy for the English to defeat the French. But the French defeated General Braddock, as we have just seen. The French continued to win most of the battles for the next two years.

How could the French win so many battles when there were so many more Englishmen? There were a number of reasons. For one thing, the French had a larger army in North America than the English had. The French had the help of many Indians. The French were also united under one government. The English had thirteen colonies, and at first the colonies did not work together very well.

In 1757 the government in England began to take more interest in the war in America. A man named William Pitt was put in charge of the war. Pitt sent more soldiers to America. He also sent some good generals. One of these generals was James Wolfe.

After 1757 the English began to win most of the battles. The English captured Fort Duquesne in 1758. George Washington fought with the army that captured Fort Duquesne. The name of the fort was changed to Fort Pitt, after William Pitt. The city that stands on this spot today is named Pittsburgh.

The English captured one fort after another, but the French still held Quebec, the capital of New France. General Wolfe decided to capture Quebec. The task seemed impossible. Quebec was a powerful fort on a high cliff above the St. Lawrence River. The French in the fort would shoot at anybody who tried to climb the cliff. The fort was in command of a brave leader,

150

General Montcalm, one of the best generals the French had.

General Wolfe had his ships sail past Quebec in the dead of night. There were no lights on the ships, so the French did not see them sailing by. When they had passed the fort, General Wolfe had his men get off the ships. He had them climb the cliff. It was a hard, dangerous climb. The men had to cling to bushes and rocks. They had to be very quiet, so the French soldiers in the fort would not hear them.

In the morning the French were surprised to find the British army just outside their fort. There was a bitter battle, but it did not last long. The British captured the fort. Both General Wolfe and General Montcalm were killed in the battle.

Quebec was captured in September, 1759. This ended the fighting in North America. The French and English were still fighting in other parts of the world, however. Finally, the French were defeated everywhere.

The peace treaty was signed in Paris in 1763.

UNEXPLORED

Hudson Bay

ENGLISH

PACIFIC OCEAN

Rocky Mountains

Missouri R.

St. Lawrence R.

FRENCH ISLANDS

NEW ENGLAND

MIDDLE COLONIES

Ohio River

SOUTHERN COLONIES

SPANISH

Mississippi River

NEW ORLEANS (Spanish)

GULF OF MEXICO

ATLANTIC OCEAN

ENGLISH	☐
SPANISH	☐
FRENCH	■
THIRTEEN COLONIES	☐

The End of the French Power in North America. When the peace treaty was signed France was forced to give up almost all her land in North America. The map shows how North America was divided by the Treaty of Paris.

1. England took Canada from France.

2. England took from France all the land east of the Mississippi River except the city of New Orleans.

3. Spain had helped France in the war, so England took Florida from Spain.

4. To pay Spain for losing Florida, France gave Spain the territory between the Mississippi River and the Rocky Mountains. France also gave Spain the city of New Orleans.

5. France was allowed to keep a few small islands near the Gulf of St. Lawrence. French fishermen used these islands for drying their fish.

France once had a great empire in North America. Now France had only a few small islands.

England once had only the thirteen colonies and some land around Hudson Bay. Now England owned almost half the continent.

The War and the Colonists. The French and Indian War had many effects upon the English colonists:

1. The colonists had always been afraid of the French. They thought that they needed the English soldiers to protect them from the French. Now the French were gone. The colonists did not think that they needed the English soldiers any longer.

2. The colonists had learned to fight as well as the English soldiers. Later, they would not be afraid to fight the English.

3. The colonists learned that war is expensive. Paying for the war caused trouble between the colonies and England.

4. The war showed the colonies that they must work together. Before the war the colonies had little to do with each other. They were jealous of one another. They had to unite to fight the French. Later, they would unite to fight the English.

In 1763 England was proud and happy. She had won a large amount of territory in North America. Within 20 years, however, she was to lose much of this territory and she was to lose most of her colonists.

A new nation was to arise in North America—the United States of America.

JEAN, A FRENCH COLONIST

Jean is a colonist in New France. His father decided to go to Canada. He wanted to make his fortune in the fur trade. He settled in Canada near the St. Lawrence River.

Like all the French colonists they are Catholics. They are farmers. They live in a little cabin on an estate owned by a lord. For the use of the land Jean must pay a small yearly rent and do some work for the lord. Farmers like Jean cannot own their own land.

If Jean or his family are sick, they will be taken to the Catholic hospital in Montreal. It is run by the Sisters. His children may go to a school and be taught by the Ursuline Sisters. They came to Quebec in 1639 to serve the Indians and white people.

Jean takes no part in making the laws of New France and he cannot vote. The colony is ruled by a governor and another man chosen by the King of France. The third leading man in the colony is the Bishop.

After the English defeated the French and Indians in a war, this part of New France was given to the English. Then many English settlers came to live in Canada. Jean and his French neighbors continued to live in peace with the new English settlers.

STUDY LESSON

WHO AM I? Write the name of each person listed. Next to it write the sentence which tells you about the person.

1. George Washington
2. La Salle
3. Edward Braddock
4. John Cabot
5. General Wolfe
6. General Montcalm

a. I laid claim to all of North America for the English.
b. I was at the head of the English army at Quebec.
c. I was sent by the Governor of Virginia to carry a message to the French in the Ohio Valley.
d. I led the French army at Quebec.
e. I claimed all the land drained by the Mississippi River for France.
f. I was used to fighting in Europe and did not know how to fight in America.

WHAT AM I? Write each name and after it the phrase that explains it.

1. Iroquois 2. Quebec 3. Florida 4. Fort Duquesne 5. New Orleans

a. captured by the English in 1758.
b. city given to Spain at the end of the French and Indian War.
c. the Indians who were on the side of the English
d. given by Spain to England.
e. the capital of New France.

SOMETHING TO THINK ABOUT. Think carefully before you answer these questions.

1. How did the French and Indian War unite the Thirteen Colonies?
2. Why did the French win most of the battles at the beginning of the French and Indian War, even though there were more English people?
3. Why was General Braddock and his army defeated by the French and Indians?
4. Why did England begin winning the French and Indian war after 1757?
5. Why was the name of Fort Duquesne changed to Fort Pitt?

DATES TO REMEMBER. Write each date in column A. Next write the phrase in column B that matches the date.

A	B
1. 1763	a. capture of Quebec.
2. 1758	b. English captured Fort Duquesne.
3. 1759	c. Treaty of Paris.

WORDS TO KNOW. Write a sentence using each of these words. Look them up in your dictionary if you are not sure of the meaning.

drained   empire   unite
treaty   continent

155

17. Bad Laws Cause Trouble

The Stamp Act Causes Excitement in the Colonies. The man on the platform in the picture is making a speech against the Stamp Act. This man lives in one of the thirteen British colonies in North America. It is the year 1765. In other colonies, there are men who are making similar speeches. Some colonists are very much excited about the Stamp Act. They think it is a bad law.

What was the Stamp Act? To answer this question we must go back two years, to 1763. In that year, the French and Indian War came to an end. In this war the British soldiers and the men living in the colonies had fought side by side. They had defeated the French who until then had owned a large part of North America. By victory in the French and Indian War, the British became the masters of North America.

The war had cost the British a huge sum of money. The British government was in debt. The members of Parliament, the British law-making body, wondered how they could pay for the war.

The members of Parliament thought that the people living in the colonies should help Britain pay for the war. "This is only fair," members of Parliament thought. "The war helped the colonists more than it helped the people of Great Britain. Because of the war the colonists are no longer in danger of being attacked by the French. They should help us pay for that war."

In 1765, therefore, Parliament

passed the Stamp Act. According to this new law the colonists had to place stamps on all important papers. The storekeeper had to stamp his bills. The banker had to stamp his checks. Even college diplomas had to be stamped. Deeds and leases to property, pamphlets, and newspapers all had to be stamped.

The Stamp Act caused great excitement in the colonies. Men made speeches against it. Newspaper articles and pamphlets said that the tax was unfair. People even attacked the houses of the tax collectors.

"Taxation without Representation." Why did the Stamp Act cause such excitement in the colonies? Did the colonists object to paying taxes for the French and Indian War?

No, the colonists did not object to paying taxes. Many of the colonists agreed that it was only fair that they should help pay for the French and Indian War. But they objected to the way they were being taxed. They wanted to make their own tax laws in their own colonial assemblies. They objected to Parliament levying their taxes.

The members of Parliament were elected by people who lived in Great Britain. The colonists lived far across the Atlantic Ocean from Great Britain. They did not elect any members to Parliament. They said it was not fair for Parliament to tax them when they had no representatives in Parliament.

"No taxation without representation!" became the slogan of the colonists. The man in the picture at the beginning of this chapter probably is saying: "No taxation without representation!"

157

For almost 150 years, many of the colonies had their own assemblies. The colonists elected the members of the assemblies. The assemblies made most of the laws for the colonies. For 150 years Parliament in London had not paid much attention to the colonies. Parliament had let the colonists rule themselves through their assemblies. Now, in 1765, Parliament was suddenly trying to become more strict with the colonists. The colonists did not like this at all.

"If we must pay more taxes, let the new tax laws be made by our own assemblies," the colonists declared.

The Stamp Act Is Repealed. Men from nine colonies met to see what could be done about the Stamp Act. This meeting was called the Stamp Act Congress. The members of this Congress sent a letter to Parliament. In the letter, they asked Parliament to remove the stamp tax. The Congress also asked the colonists to stop buying from British merchants until the tax was removed.

The Stamp Act Congress was important because it showed that men from the different colonies could work together. Until the time of the French and Indian War, the colonies had not had much to do with each other. They were jealous of each other, and they sometimes quarreled with each other. Now the colonists were working together.

The colonists did as the Stamp Act Congress requested. They stopped buying from British merchants. These merchants lost so much business that they begged Parliament to repeal the Stamp Act. Parliament did so in 1766. The colonists were happy. They thought they had won a great victory.

Parliament still insisted, however, that it had the right to tax the colonists any time it wished.

New Taxes Bring More Trouble. King George III of England was very angry when the Stamp Act was repealed. George III was a stubborn man. He was not a wise ruler. He was determined to show the colonists that they must obey the British government.

In 1767, the king's friends in Parliament passed a new tax which they said the colonists must pay. This tax was on lead, glass, paint, and tea.

Once again there was great excitement in the colonies. Once again the colonists cried: "No taxation without representation!" Samuel Adams and other colonial leaders told the colonists not to buy any of the articles that were taxed.

"The Boston Massacre." The people of Boston were especially excited about the new taxes. The British were afraid there would be trouble in Boston. So they sent some soldiers there to keep law and order.

The people of Boston were more angry than ever when they saw the soldiers. "Great Britain is treating us as if we were a conquered country," many Boston people said.

One day in 1770 there was trouble between some of the people and a band of soldiers. The people threw snowballs at the soldiers and hit the soldiers with sticks. After a time, the angry soldiers raised their guns and fired. Several persons were killed and a few wounded.

Excitement was greater than ever now. The news spread throughout the thirteen colonies. People called this event the "Boston Massacre." "Massacre" means the cruel killing of people who are not able to defend themselves.

There might have been more trouble, but just at this time, Parliament repealed most of the new taxes. The colonists were pleased about this, and their anger cooled somewhat.

Parliament kept just one tax. That was the tax on tea. King George III said: "We must keep a tax on something to show that we have a right to tax the colonies."

Committees of Correspondence. Samuel Adams knew that the Americans must work together to resist the harsh British laws. When something important happened in one town the people of other towns should know about it. People who lived in different places should also exchange ideas as to what they could do about the British laws.

After the Boston Massacre, Samuel Adams formed a Committee of Correspondence in Boston. This committee sent newsletters by special messengers to all near-by towns. The idea spread. Committees of Correspondence were formed in all the colonies. These Committees sent letters back and forth. In this way, the people of each colony knew what was going on in other colonies. Americans felt they were united in resisting the British.

The Boston Tea Party. In 1773, several shiploads of tea were sent to various colonies. The English tea merchants made the price of the tea very low. Even with the tax added, tea was cheaper in America than it was in England. This was done because King George III wished to trick the colonists into buying the tea and paying the tax. But the colonists were not so easily tricked. In most of the cities the colonists would not permit the tea to be landed. The ships turned around and sailed back to England.

The matter was not settled so easily in Boston. There the royal governor refused to allow the tea to be returned to England. He did not wish to give in to the colonists. He felt this would be a sign of weakness.

The matter was finally settled in a most unusual way. Sixty colonists, dressed as Indians, climbed aboard the ships which were loaded with tea. They chopped open the 342 chests and threw the tea and the tea chests into the water. This was called the Boston Tea Party.

The Boston Tea Party was an unjust act, because the tea which was destroyed belonged to English merchants. The colonists had no quarrel with these merchants. Their quarrel was with the king and with Parliament.

Boston Is Punished. The Boston Tea Party made the British angry. The owners had lost their tea and the government had lost its tax. Worst of all, the people of Boston had defied the British government. King George III and his friends in Parliament decided that the people of Boston must be taught to obey.

In 1774, the port of Boston was closed. No ships were allowed to sail in or out of the port. This was very harsh punishment because many people in Boston depended upon ships and shipping for their living. The business of merchants and shipowners was ruined and many sailors were out of work.

The Committees of Correspondence got to work. The word spread through the colonies: "The port of Boston is closed. The people of Boston need help." The people of other colonies sent food overland to Boston so that the people of that city would not go hungry.

The king sent a new governor to Massachusetts. The new governor was also a general. His name was General Thomas Gage, and he was in charge of 5,000 soldiers.

General Gage told the members of the Massachusetts Assembly that they were no longer allowed to meet. This was a great blow. The people of Massachusetts were proud of their assembly. Without an assembly they would no longer be a self-governing people.

The Assembly did not obey the governor's order. It met in secret. The members of the assembly planned to arm the colonists and to fight if necessary.

The First Continental Congress. The colonists talked more and more about their troubles with Great Britain. Through the Committees of Correspondence, the people in different colonies exchanged ideas about the problem. The colonists decided that there should be a meeting of men from the various colonies. This meeting began in Philadelphia on September 5, 1774. It is called the First Continental Congress. Men from every colony except Georgia were there. Some of the leaders who were at the meeting were Samuel Adams, Patrick Henry, John Adams, George Washington, and Benjamin Franklin.

The members of the First Continental Congress drew up a list of the things the colonists were complaining about. This list was sent to England. The Congress also agreed that the colonists would not buy anything from England or sell anything to England, until their troubles had been settled.

Until this time, the colonies had not been united. A colonist did not think of himself as an American. He thought of himself as a Virginian, or a New Yorker, or a New Englander. Patrick Henry knew it was necessary for the colonists to forget their differences and to work together. During the first meeting of this Congress he said: "The distinctions between Virginians and Pennsylvanians, New Yorkers and New Englanders, are no more. I am not a Virginian, but an American."

Paul Revere's Ride. The colonists of Massachusetts got together a supply of guns, powder, and shot. These supplies were hidden at Concord, near Boston.

Companies of men gathered secretly and drilled as soldiers. They were called Minute Men, because they were ready to fight at a minute's notice.

Despite the care to keep these things secret, the British learned what was going on. General Gage planned to send some soldiers to Concord to seize the colonists' supplies. The night before the soldiers were ready to march, Paul Revere and William Dawes rode through the countryside. At the home of every Minute Man they pounded on the door and shouted, "The British are coming!" The Minute Men dressed quickly, seized their guns, and rode off. This was on the night of April 18, 1775.

The Shot "Heard Round the World." The next morning the British soldiers marched from Boston. Their red coats were dazzling in the sun. At the little town of Lexington they found a small band of Minute Men waiting for them.

Captain John Parker of the Minute Men said to his soldiers: "Stand your ground! Don't fire unless fired upon, but if they mean to have war let it begin here."

Major John Pitcairn, the British commander called out: "Disperse, ye rebels, disperse!"

Not a man moved.

The English commander then gave the order "Fire!" Eight Minute Men fell dead. They were the first men killed in our war for independence.

The British marched on six more miles to Concord. They burned the courthouse and seized what supplies were left. At a bridge on the edge of town, the British met another group of Minute Men. Another short battle was fought.

As the British soldiers marched back to Boston, the colonists fired at them from behind every stone, tree, and bush. Before the British reached Boston, nearly 300 of them had been killed, wounded, or captured.

The poet, Ralph Waldo Emerson, described the fighting at Concord in these words:

> By the rude bridge that arched the flood,
> Their flag to April's breeze unfurled,
> Here once the embattled farmers stood,
> And fired the shot heard round the world.

The Capture of Ticonderoga. The Committees of Correspondence quickly spread the news throughout the colonies. "Fighting has begun!" they said. Bands of colonists from Connecticut and Massachusetts took up arms and joined the "Green Mountain Boys" from Vermont. This force, led by Ethan Allen, made a surprise attack on Fort Ticonderoga in New York. The British surrendered the fort. The Americans found valuable cannons and ammunition in the surrendered fort. The Americans needed these supplies.

The Battle of Bunker Hill. The Americans wished to drive General Gage's soldiers out of Boston. They fortified Bunker Hill and Breed's Hill, two heights which overlook the city of Boston and Boston Harbor.

General Gage knew that the British would not be able to stay in Boston if the Americans held these heights. He ordered his men to drive the American off Breed's Hill.

Three thousand British soldiers were brought to the foot of the hill. Up they charged, shoulder to shoulder. Not a gun was fired until they came to within a few yards of the Americans. Then came a killing fire from the Americans. The British fell back.

A second charge was made. Again, the same killing fire.

A last desperate attempt was made. This time the Americans ran out of ammunition and had to retreat.

The British won the battle, but the Americans had shown that they were very good fighters.

Although this battle was fought on Breed's Hill, it is called the Battle of Bunker Hill.

Washington Drives the British From Boston. The Second Continental Congress met for the first time in May, 1775. Delegates from all the colonies except Georgia were present.

The Second Continental Congress voted to make George Washington Commander-in-Chief of the American forces. Washington went to Massachusetts, where the Americans were trying to drive the British from Boston. Washington took command of his army on July 3, 1775.

In January, Washington received the cannons and ammunition which had been captured at Fort Ticonderoga. Washington seized Dorchester Heights. The cannons were placed on this hill and pointed directly at the city of Boston. The British saw that they could no longer hold the city. In March, 1776, they sailed away.

George Washington and his American soldiers marched into Boston. The people of Boston cheered George Washington. They were happy to be free once more.

The Colonists Declare Their Independence. When the Second Continental Congress first met, the members did not think about breaking away from Great Britain. They were willing to be part of the British Empire, but they wanted better treatment.

As time went on, some members of Congress saw that they could not expect fair treatment from King George III or from his friends in Parliament. They finally decided that they must break away from Great Britain.

Congress asked Thomas Jefferson and some other delegates to write a statement saying that the colonies no longer belonged to Great Britain. This statement is called the Declaration of Independence. Independence means freedom. Jefferson did almost all the writing.

The Declaration of Independence proclaims that all men are created equal. It states that all men have certain rights which no government can take away from them. Catholic scholars had taught these ideas for more than a thousand years.

The Declaration then says that the British king had attempted to take away many of the rights of the colonists. It says that the colonies were, therefore, declaring themselves independent of Great Britain. From that time on, the colonies would be the United States of America.

On July 4, 1776, the members of the Second Continental Congress voted to adopt the Declaration.

July 4 is the birthday of the United States. On that day, in 1776, the United States of America was born.

STUDY LESSON

WHAT IS IT? Write each name and after it the phrase that explains it.

1. Stamp Act
2. colonial assemblies
3. Boston Massacre
4. Committees of Correspondence
5. Boston Tea Party
6. First Continental Congress
7. Minute Men
8. Green Mountain Boys
9. Second Continental Congress
10. Declaration of Independence

a. delegates from the colonies who met in Philadelphia in 1774 to discuss how to deal with England
b. the killing of Boston people by British soldiers in 1770
c. adopted by Second Continental Congress, July 4, 1776
d. a law made by England to raise money to pay for the French and Indian War
e. made George Washington Commander-in-Chief
f. groups organized by Samuel Adams
g. name given to the soldiers of Vermont
h. destruction of tea shipment by Boston colonists
i. colonists who took military training and were ready to fight whenever needed
j. made most of the laws for the colonies

WHO AM I? Write each name and after it the phrase that tells something about him.

1. George III
2. Captain Parker
3. Thomas Jefferson
4. General Gage
5. Major Pitcairn
6. Patrick Henry

a. British commander at the battle of Lexington
b. King of England during our struggle for independence
c. wrote most of the Declaration of Independence
d. leader of the Minute Men at the Battle of Lexington
e. said: "I am not a Virginian but an American."
f. Governor of Boston when the American Revolution started

SOMETHING TO THINK ABOUT. Think carefully before you answer these questions.

1. What was the chief cause of trouble between England and the colonies?
2. Why did England pass the Stamp Act?
3. Explain why the colonies objected to the Stamp Act.
4. After the Boston Massacre, how did Samuel Adams help unite the colonies?

18. Americans Win Their Freedom

The War for Freedom. By July, 1776, George Washington had been Commander-in-Chief of the American forces for more than a year. During this time, he and his men had been fighting for their rights as free men. They were not yet fighting for independence from the King of England.

Then, in July, 1776, George Washington learned that the Continental Congress had adopted the Declaration of Independence. Washington was happy when he read the Declaration of Independence. He had it read to his men. In the picture above, the American soldiers have just heard the Declaration of Independence for the first time. Now they have something new to fight for. Now they are fighting for their country, the United States of America.

Our country's first war is sometimes called the War for Independence. Independence meant freedom from Great Britain's rule. Many people also call it the Revolutionary War, or the American Revolution. The word "revolution" means change. This war brought about a big change for Americans.

Washington Is Driven From New York. The British at first thought that General Washington could easily be defeated. Great Britain at that time was the most powerful country in the world. The British had a strong army and the world's most powerful navy. Washington had an army of farmers who had very little training for war. His men did not have enough guns, enough ammunition, or enough food. Washington had no navy at all when the war started.

Washington was in New York City with an army that sometimes numbered only 11,000 men. The British decided to take New York City. There were two reasons why the city would be valuable to the British. In the first place New York has the best harbor along the Atlantic coast. If the British held the city of New York, their ships would be able to use the harbor. The second reason was that New York stood between New England and the Southern colonies. If the British held New York, it would be easier for them to cut the United States in two.

The British attacked New York City with a force of 35,000 men. This was more than three times as many men as Washington could depend upon. For a time, it looked as if Washington's army would be captured. But Washington was able to escape. He took his army into New Jersey.

The British entered New York City. They held this city till the end of the war.

Nathan Hale Gives His Life. After Washington was driven from New York, he wished to find out what the British planned to do next. He asked if someone would go into the British camp and try to get this information. A young officer named Captain Nathan Hale volunteered.

Captain Hale pretended to be a schoolmaster. He went into the British camp. He found out what the British were planning to do next. He started back to the American lines to tell Washington what he had learned. Before he had gone far, someone recognized him. He was arrested.

Nathan Hale had been spying on the British, and in times of war spies are usually put to death. Hale was sentenced to be hanged. As the rope was put around his neck, he said: "I only regret that I have but one life to give for my country."

Washington Retreats Across New Jersey. After he was defeated in New York, General Washington retreated across the State of New Jersey. He was followed by General

Cornwallis with a fine British army. When Washington reached the Delaware River, his men took all the boats they could find. They sank the boats they could not use. Then they crossed the river into Pennsylvania.

The British could not cross the river because they had no boats. Cornwallis decided to return to New York until the river froze. Then he was sure his men could easily cross the river and defeat Washington. At Trenton, New Jersey, Cornwallis left a force to watch Washington. These soldiers were Hessians, or Germans who had been hired to fight for the British.

When Washington first entered New York City he had about 11,000 men. Later, some of these men were killed or wounded. Others went back to their farms. When he reached Pennsylvania, Washington had only 3,000 men left. Their clothes were in tatters. Their shoes were worn. They had little ammunition, and they were half starved.

It did not seem possible that Washington's army could last much longer. It looked as if the war were almost over.

Washington Wins Two Big Battles. Christmas night, 1776, was wild and stormy. There was a piercing wind and a heavy snow storm. This was the night Washington selected to attack the Hessians at Trenton. His men crossed the Delaware River in their small boats. The river was full of huge cakes of floating ice, but not a boat was lost. After the men crossed the river they marched nine miles to Trenton.

The Hessians were taken completely by surprise. They surrendered after a short battle.

General Cornwallis heard about this battle and rushed from New York with another army. Cornwallis left three regiments at Princeton and went on to Trenton with his main army. Washington slipped away from the main British army and captured the three regiments at Princeton.

Cornwallis was now in danger of being cut off from the ocean, his source of supply. He hurried back to New York. He left all of New Jersey in Washington's hands.

The two victories at Trenton and Princeton showed the British that the war would not be over as soon as they had thought.

The Famous Victory at Saratoga. The war had been dragging on for two years. Then the British thought they had a plan at last which would really defeat the Americans. Under this plan, three British armies were to meet at Albany, New York. The first army was to come down from Canada. A second force was to go up from New York City. The third was to come across the Mohawk Valley from Lake Ontario. When the three armies met at Albany, New England would be cut off from the other states. Then each section could be conquered separately.

The plan did not work out. The army that was to cross the Mohawk Valley was beaten by the Americans at Fort Stanwix. The army that was to march north from New York to Albany went to Philadelphia instead.

General Burgoyne led the main army down from Montreal. As he marched through the forest, Americans shot at him from behind stones and trees. The Americans also kept Burgoyne's men from getting any food. His men were already tired and hungry when they were surrounded at Saratoga, New York. Burgoyne surrendered on October 17, 1777.

This American victory meant more than just winning a battle.

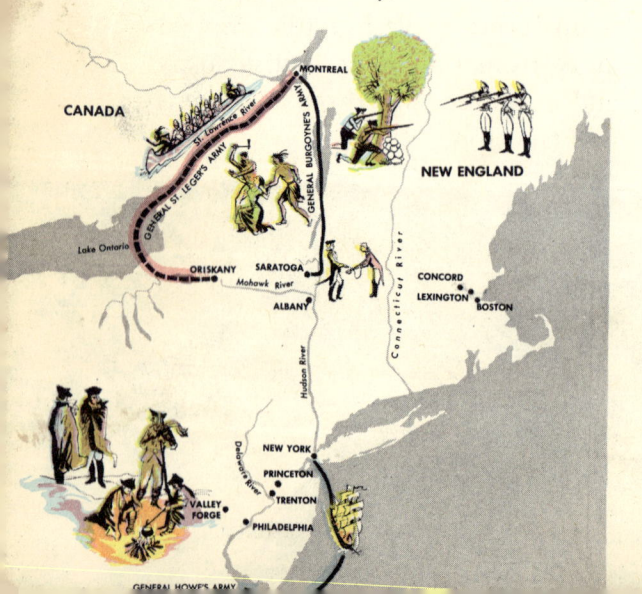

France had been wishing to come into the war on the American side and already had secretly helped us. Now, France saw that the Americans had a good chance of winning the war. After the Battle of Saratoga, France agreed to help the Americans with an army and a fleet.

Later, Spain and Holland also declared war against Great Britain.

A Severe Winter at Valley Forge. In the fall of 1777 Washington led his army into Valley Forge, Pennsylvania. Here the army set up winter quarters. In those days it was the custom to do as little fighting as possible in winter.

The men lived in rude shacks. The winter was terribly cold, and the shacks did not give them much protection from the weather. There was very little food. The horses starved to death. Men had to be harnessed to wagons to bring in the food. Most of the soldiers were very poorly clothed. Many of them had no shoes.

Washington saw all this, and it nearly broke his heart. He prayed for help, and he never gave up hope.

John Barry of the American Navy. The Americans had no navy when the war began. The Americans allowed merchant ships to carry guns and capture English ships. These merchant ships were called privateers. They did great damage to British shipping.

Later, the Americans built a small navy. Captain John Barry became the first officer in this navy. Barry had been born in Ireland and was a Catholic. When the American Revolution broke out he asked Congress to let him fight for the United States. He was given an old ship named the *Lexington*. The *Lexington* captured the *Edward,* a large British warship.

After this victory, Barry went to

Philadelphia. He was given a new ship, but the ship was not yet ready. While he was waiting, Barry thought of a plan to capture some British ships on the Delaware River. These ships were stopping all American boats and were also bringing supplies to the British.

Barry started down the Delaware River at night with four boatloads of men. Rags were put in the oarlocks so that not a sound was heard. At sunrise they were alongside a British warship. Barry's men were on the decks of the British vessel in a few minutes. The British were taken by surprise and surrendered. Barry then captured four British supply ships almost as easily as he had captured the warship.

John Paul Jones. John Paul Jones was another great American naval officer. Jones was born in Scotland. He came to America when he was a young man and fought for the United States in the Revolution. He fought bravely on several ships. He was such a daring seaman that he even sailed close to the coast of England. There he sank several ships.

Jones was in command of an old broken-down French ship, the *Bon Homme Richard*. He found himself in a battle with the fine British warship, the *Serapis*. The cannons of the British ship tore big holes in the rotten sides of Jones' vessel.

The captain of the British ship shouted to Captain Jones to surrender.

Jones answered: "I have not yet begun to fight."

After a fierce fight, the British surrendered. Jones and his crew then worked with might and main to move their wounded men onto the captured British ship. Just as they moved the last man aboard, the *Bon Homme Richard* sank.

George Rogers Clark in Ohio. The Ohio Valley was rich country. France had lost this country to the English in the French and Indian War. Now, George Rogers Clark made up his mind to conquer it for the Americans. There were few settlements in the territory. The English had Fort Kaskaskia on the Mississippi River and Fort Vincennes near the Wabash River. Clark knew that if he could capture these forts the whole Ohio country would belong to the Americans.

Clark gathered a force of 200 men to capture Kaskaskia. He knew that to succeed he must take the fort by surprise. The British were having a dance at the fort. They did not dream that there was an American within miles. Clark slipped into the hall where the dance was being held. He told the British that the fort was now in American hands. He had captured the fort without firing a shot.

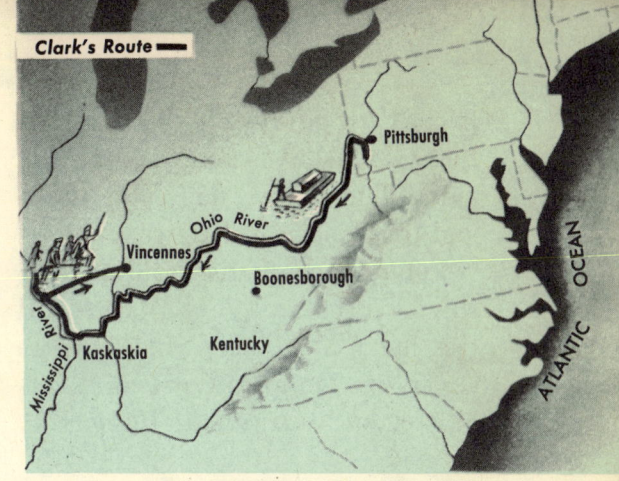

Father Pierre Gibault was present at the surrender of Kaskaskia. He liked the Americans. Father Gibault went to Vincennes, which was 200 miles away. Most of the people there were French and they were Catholics. Father Gibault told the people that the Americans were fighting the British. He also told them that the Americans were their friends. The people agreed that they would live under American rule. The British flag came down and the American flag went up.

Later, some British soldiers captured Vincennes. When Clark heard this he decided he would have to re-capture the fort. Once more, his only chance was to take the fort by surprise.

Clark knew that the British would not be expecting an attack in the middle of winter. He and his men marched more than 200 miles. Often they walked through icy water. The British were not ready for an attack, and they surrendered after a short fight.

All the Ohio country was now in the hands of the Americans. When the treaty of peace was signed, this territory was given to the United States. It became known as the Northwest Territory. Five states have been made out of this territory. They are Ohio, Indiana, Illinois, Michigan, and Wisconsin.

Arnold Betrays His Country. When France joined the war against Great Britain she sent a large fleet to America. The British heard that the fleet was coming, and they decided to give up Philadelphia. The British army hurried across New Jersey toward New York. Washington defeated them at the Battle of Monmouth, but he was not able to destroy the army.

The Americans also won other battles in the Middle States. "Mad Anthony" Wayne captured Stony Point on the Hudson. "Light Horse Harry" Lee took Paulus Hook on New York Bay.

While the Americans were winning these battles, something happened that made George Washington sad. Benedict Arnold, one of America's finest officers, betrayed his country.

Arnold had fought bravely for the Americans at the beginning of the war. The American victory in the Battle of Saratoga was largely due to the courage of Benedict Arnold.

Then Arnold decided that Congress was not treating him justly. He also owed many debts. He had a plan which he thought would help him get "revenge" against his country and at the same time get him out of debt. General Arnold was in charge of the important fort at West Point on the Hudson River. He offered to sell this fort to the British.

The Americans found out about Arnold's plan and arrested Major André, the British officer who had been plotting with Arnold. Major André was hanged as a spy. Benedict Arnold escaped to England. There he learned that the British had nothing but contempt for a man who would betray his country. Benedict Arnold died in London in misery and loneliness.

Friends From Other Countries. Many liberty-loving men from other countries came to America to help us fight the Revolution. The brave Marquis de Lafayette came from France. Washington greatly esteemed the young Frenchman. He made Lafayette a major general in the American Army.

Baron Johann de Kalb came from Bavaria. He shared the hardships of Valley Forge with the Americans. He died in battle.

Baron von Steuben came from Prussia. He drilled the American soldiers and taught them how to act in battle.

Thaddeus Kosciusko came from Poland. He was an engineer and showed the Americans how to build forts and bridges.

Casimir Pulaski, another Pole, organized the American cavalry. He died as a result of wounds received in battle.

Lafayette, Kosciusko, and Pulaski were all Catholics.

The War in the South. The English had been defeated in the North, so they turned to the South. There they were successful for some time. General Cornwallis captured Savannah, in Georgia, and Charleston, in South Carolina.

The Americans had no large armies in the South, but they did have a number of small forces. These little groups would attack Cornwallis and then disappear into the forest. Later, they would come back and attack again. Today, we call this type of fighting guerrilla warfare.

These constant attacks wore out the British army. Cornwallis took his army to Yorktown, on the seacoast. Here, he waited for fresh men and fresh supplies from England.

This was the chance Washington had been waiting for.

The War Ends. Washington marched to Yorktown with his army. Many French soldiers went there, too. A large French fleet sailed to Yorktown and cut off Cornwallis by sea. Cornwallis was completely surrounded. There was nothing he could do but surrender. He did so on October 18, 1781.

"It is all over," said a leader of the British government when he heard that Cornwallis had surrendered.

King George III wanted to keep on fighting. He still hoped to conquer the United States. But the British people wanted no more war. The fighting ended when Cornwallis surrendered.

The peace treaty was signed two years later, on September 3, 1783. In the peace treaty, Great Britain agreed that the United States was "a free and independent nation." The country extended from the Atlantic Ocean to the Mississippi River.

Washington Leaves the Army. George Washington left the army on December 23, 1783. He was sorry to leave the men who had served him for more than eight years. But he was happy to be going back to his beautiful home at Mount Vernon.

As Washington said goodbye to the men, he did not know that his country would call upon him again. He did not know of the great task that lay ahead.

STUDY LESSON

WHERE IS IT? Answer each question in a complete sentence.

1. What river did Washington cross when retreating from the British?
2. Where were the Hessians encamped when they were attacked by Washington's soldiers?
3. Where did Washington capture the three regiments left behind by Cornwallis?
4. Where did the Americans defeat Burgoyne?
5. Where is Valley Forge?
6. Where did the British suffer their final defeat of the war?

WHO AM I? Write the name of each person listed. Next to it write the phrase which tells you about the person.

1. Nathan Hale
2. John Barry
3. John Paul Jones
4. George Rogers Clark
5. Benedict Arnold
6. Major André
7. "Mad Anthony" Wayne
8. Marquis de Lafayette
9. Baron von Steuben
10. Thaddeus Kosciusko
11. Casimir Pulaski

a. Polish officer who organized the American cavalry
b. British officer who plotted to seize West Point
c. Prussian who helped drill the American army
d. the man known for his reply: "I have not yet begun to fight!"
e. the patriot who said: "I only regret that I have but one life to give for my country."
f. Polish engineer who taught the American army to build bridges and fortifications
g. a brave Frenchman who fought on the American side
h. the American officer who betrayed his country.
i. the American officer who captured Stony Point on the Hudson
j. the conqueror of the Northwest Territory
k. first officer in the American Navy

WORDS TO KNOW. Use each of these words in a sentence. Look them up in your dictionary unless you are sure of their meaning.

independence declaration
privateers guerrilla warfare

SOMETHING TO THINK ABOUT. Think carefully before you answer these questions.

1. Why was the capture of New York important to the British?
2. Why did Washington ask Nathan Hale to go to New York?
3. Why was Washington's attack on Trenton so successful?
4. Do you know of another attack in that war which was successful for the same reason?
5. Why was the American victory at Saratoga so important?
6. How did Captain John Barry capture the British ships at Philadelphia?
7. Why do you think many officers came from Europe to help the Americans?

WHEN DID IT HAPPEN? Match the time with the event.

A	B
1763	Boston Tea Party
1773	Declaration of Independence
1774	French and Indian War ends
1776	First Continental Congress
1781	Revolutionary War ends

Unit Five

EARLY DAYS OF OUR REPUBLIC

19. The States Form a Strong Union

The Constitutional Convention. The men in this picture are having a very important meeting. They are meeting in Philadelphia in May, 1787. This is five and a half years after the American Revolution came to an end. It is three and a half years since the Treaty of Peace was signed in Paris, France. In that treaty Great Britain agreed that the thirteen American colonies no longer belonged to her. Now they are free and independent states.

Who are these men? They are men sent from the different states. Why are these men having a meeting? They want to form a strong union of the thirteen states.

Ever since the fighting came to an end, the thirteen states have been like thirteen little nations. Each state has members in Congress, but Congress does not have much power. For example, Congress cannot raise money; it has to ask the states for it. Some states have made commerce

Rhode Island sent men to a meeting in Philadelphia in May, 1787. These men were supposed to find a way for the states to form a united country and to frame a constitution for this united country. A constitution contains the basic laws or rules of a country. We call this meeting the Constitutional Convention.

The Constitutional Convention had fifty-five members. Two of the members, Thomas Fitz-Simons of Pennsylvania and Daniel Carroll of Maryland, were Catholics.

George Washington was one of those present at the meeting. He was sent by his own state, Virginia. All the other members elected George Washington President of the Convention. That is why he is standing by the chair at the head of the room.

How Many Congressmen? The members of the Constitutional Convention agreed that there should be a federal Congress or law-making body to make laws for the people of all the states. But how many men should each state send to Congress?

The members from the large states said: "The states with the most people should have the most Congressmen. That is only fair."

"No," said the members from the small states. "If that happened the small states would always be out-

laws which are harmful to other states. There have been disputes about boundaries, and about many other things.

Thoughtful men have been worried.

"We cannot go on like this," they said. "If the states continue to quarrel among themselves a united country will be impossible. Then it will be easy for some other country to conquer us. The thirteen states must unite. We must form one united country."

That is why all the states except

179

voted. We would be ruled by the large states. We shall not agree to such a plan."

For a time it looked as if the members of the convention would never agree on this point. It looked as if the convention would be a failure.

Benjamin Franklin, who was a delegate from Pennsylvania, rose to his feet. He begged the other members to ask for God's help. "I have lived a long time," Franklin said, "and the longer I live the more convincing proofs I see of this: that God governs in the affairs of man."

Franklin reminded the other delegates that even a sparrow cannot fall to the ground unless God lets it fall. How then, Franklin asked, could a great nation arise without God's help?

The members paused and bowed their heads in prayer.

Not long after seeking God's help the delegates were able to agree on a plan for Congress. This was the plan: Congress would have two houses. There would be the House of Representatives and the Senate. In the House of Representatives the states with the most people would have the most members. In the Senate every state would have two members no matter what its size.

This plan satisfied both the big states and the small states. It is the plan we still follow today.

Strong States or Strong Country? Each of the thirteen states had its own government. This is called the state government.

The government for the whole country is called the federal government. How strong should the federal government be? This was another problem that faced the members of the Constitutional Convention.

"The federal government should be very strong," said some of the members. "Experience proves it. That is why we are having this meeting. We want to form a strong union. We already have had enough trouble with a weak federal government."

"But the federal government must not have too much power," said other members. "If it is too strong, it might take away the rights of the states. Not long ago we fought a war with England. We believed that the government in London was taking away our liberties by exercising too much power."

Powers of the Government. After they talked about this for a long time, the members of the Convention wrote down what powers the federal government should have and what powers it should not have. They wrote down what powers the state governments should not have. The states were not allowed to coin money, for example. The states were not allowed to make treaties with foreign countries or to declare war. Only the federal government could do these things.

But the state governments still had much power. The states control the qualifications for voting. The states decide how much authority city, town, and county governments may have. The state lawmakers draw up their own laws on education, business, and industry inside the state. The states hold courts, punish crimes, build roads, keep birth and death records, and do many other things.

Most of the members were satisfied with this plan. The federal government was strong enough to give the states a strong union, but it was not strong enough to destroy the states.

Three Branches of Government. The members of the Constitutional Convention gave us a federal government with three branches, the executive, the judicial, and the legislative.

The members of the Constitutional Convention found it hard to agree on many points. They met almost every day for the whole summer. Finally they agreed on all major points and drew up a plan for the government of the United States. This plan is called the United States Constitution.

THE THREE BRANCHES OF GOVERNMENT

1. The President sees that the laws are carried out. In other words, he executes them. He is the head of the *executive* branch of the government.

2. The Supreme Court and other federal courts explain the laws. Explaining the law is called a *judicial* act. The courts are the *judicial* branch of the government.

3. Congress makes the laws. Those who make the laws are said to legislate. Therefore Congress is the *legislative* branch of the government.

Accepting the Constitution. The members of the Constitutional Convention had written the Constitution. But the Constitution would not become the law of the land unless the states accepted it.

Would the states accept the Constitution? Would the United States really have a strong government, or would there still be thirteen little quarreling states?

The members of the Constitutional Convention went back to their own states. They made speeches about the Constitution. They wrote newspaper articles about it.

"If we do not adopt the Constitution our country will never be strong," these leaders said to the people. "We may even be conquered by another country and lose our freedom."

Other men made speeches against the Constitution. Some of those who were against the Constitution were afraid to accept it because one very important thing had been left out. The Constitution did not say in black and white that every man would have certain rights such as freedom of religion, freedom of speech, freedom of assembly, a free press, etc.

One state after another voted to accept the Constitution, on condition that amendments be immediately drawn up listing the rights of every American citizen. These are the first ten amendments of the Constitution. They are called the Bill of Rights. The Constitution became the law of the land in 1788. The Bill of Rights was added in 1791.

Some other changes have been made in the Constitution since then, but it is still the same Constitution. Today we have forty-eight states instead of thirteen, and we may soon have forty-nine or fifty. We have 160 million people instead of 3 million. But we still have the same government that was founded by the Constitutional Convention in 1787.

The members of that convention did their work well.

STUDY LESSON

WHERE IS IT? Answer each question in a complete sentence.

1. Where was the Treaty of Peace of 1783 signed?
2. Where did the Constitutional Convention meet in 1787?
3. From which state did Thomas FitzSimons come?
4. From which state did George Washington come?

WORDS TO KNOW. Use each of these words in a sentence. Look them up in your dictionary, unless you are sure of their meaning.

federal	congress
judicial	delegate
independent	representative
legislative	senate
executive	

WHAT IS IT? Write each name and after it the phrase that explains it.

1. Congress
2. Constitutional Convention
3. federal government
4. Constitution
5. legislative branch
6. judicial branch
7. executive branch
8. Bill of Rights

a. the part of our Constitution which lists our freedoms
b. the government for the whole united country
c. the basic federal law of our country
d. the branch of government which makes the laws
e. the meeting which made the federal law of our land
f. the branch of government which explains the law
g. the body of men which makes laws for the people of all the states
h. the branch of government which sees to it that the laws are carried out

WHO AM I? Write each name and after it the phrase that tells about him.

1. George Washington
2. Thomas Fitz-Simons
3. Daniel Carroll
4. Benjamin Franklin

a. a Catholic member of the Constitutional Convention who came from Pennsylvania
b. the man who was elected President of the Constitutional Convention
c. the Catholic delegate sent by Maryland
d. the Pennsylvania delegate who begged the other members to ask for God's help

SOMETHING TO THINK ABOUT. Think carefully before you answer these questions.

1. Why did the Convention members decide on two houses of Congress?
2. What are some of the powers which the Constitutional Convention gave to the federal government? Name some powers which the federal government is denied. Were the powers of the federal government written down in the Constitution?
3. What powers do the state governments have? What powers do they not have?
4. Why does our federal government need three branches?
5. When the members of the Constitutional Convention finished writing the Constitution why did it not at once become the law of the land? What had still to be done to make it the law?
6. When was the Bill of Rights adopted? What are these rights?

20. George Washington, the First President

President Washington. You can probably tell that the man in this picture is George Washington. He is on his way from his home in Virginia to the city of New York. It is April, 1789. When he arrives in New York, George Washington will become the first President of the United States.

In the last chapter we read that the states adopted the United States Constitution. It became the law of the land in 1788. The Constitution said that the United States should have a Congress, a Supreme Court, and a President.

When it was time to elect a President, George Washington received every vote.

Washington was living at his country home in Virginia. He loved this home and did not wish to leave it. But his country wanted him to be President, so he thought it was his duty to accept. He left his home and rode to New York on horseback. This trip took several days. Every time he went through a town, the people came out to cheer him, as we see in the picture above.

It is no wonder the people loved George Washington. He had served his country well. He fought in the French and Indian War. He led the American forces in the Revolution. He had served as President of the Constitutional Convention. Now he was going to serve his nation again.

Washington Takes His Oath. Today, the President of the United States lives in the city of Washington, D. C. You may wonder why George Washington went to New York to become President.

In those days there was no city of Washington. New York City was then the capital of the United States. That is why Washington went to New York.

On April 30, 1789, Washington took his oath of office on the balcony of Federal Hall in New York City. Thousands of people stood in the street and listened.

Washington put his hand on the open Bible and said: "I solemnly swear that I will faithfully execute the office of President of the United States and will, to the best of my ability, preserve, protect, and defend the Constitution of the United States."

As Washington turned to kiss the Bible, guns were fired in a salute to him. The people in the street shouted, "Long live George Washington, the President of the United States."

Washington's Helpers. George Washington asked some men to be his helpers. These men were called his cabinet. Every President has a cabinet. Today, there are ten men in the cabinet. Washington had only four men in his cabinet.

These are the names of the four men who were in Washington's cabinet: Henry Knox, Edmund Randolph, Alexander Hamilton, and Thomas Jefferson.

Henry Knox became Secretary of War. This meant that he was to take charge of the army and navy. Knox had been one of Washington's officers during the Revolutionary War.

Edmund Randolph became Attorney General. Randolph was a Virginia lawyer. The Attorney General has to be a lawyer because his work is with the law. You might say that he is the lawyer for the government.

Thomas Jefferson became Secretary of State. His duty was to take charge of all business with foreign governments. You have read about Thomas Jefferson before. As you remember, he wrote the Declaration of Independence. You will read a great deal more about him later.

Alexander Hamilton was perhaps the most helpful member of Washington's cabinet. Hamilton became Secretary of the Treasury. This meant that he was in charge of the country's money affairs. This was a very difficult job. During the Revolution the Continental Congress had borrowed much money. The states had also borrowed money. Now this money had to be paid back. It was Hamilton's job to raise the money that was needed to pay the debts.

HENRY KNOX

EDMUND RANDOLPH

THOMAS JEFFERSON

ALEXANDER HAMILTON

Alexander Hamilton. Alexander Hamilton was born on one of the islands of the West Indies. His family was so poor that he had to go to work when he was twelve years old. Whenever he found time the young man studied. He wrote some fine articles for the newspapers.

A number of people became interested in the young man because he could write so well. They thought he should have a chance to go to school. They collected some money and sent him to New York. He went to King's College in New York. This is now Columbia University.

At the outbreak of the American Revolution, Hamilton joined the patriots and became a captain in the American army. General Washington heard of Hamilton's fine work and sent for him. Hamilton became a member of Washington's staff. This means he was one of the officers who advised General Washington. For a while Hamilton was Washington's secretary. Then Hamilton went back to fighting again. He was a very brave soldier. At Yorktown he led the final charge against the British.

After the Revolution Hamilton became a lawyer. He made many speeches and wrote many articles about the Constitution. It was largely because of Hamilton that New York accepted the Constitution.

We have seen that Hamilton became Secretary of the Treasury when Washington became President. He was only thirty-two years old at that time. He did a fine job as Secretary of the Treasury and succeeded in paying off many of the country's debts.

The First Political Parties. Thomas Jefferson and Alexander Hamilton were both members of President Washington's cabinet. The two men were different in almost every way.

Thomas Jefferson was born rich. Nevertheless, he worked all his life for the poor people. He believed that the people should control the government.

Hamilton was born poor, but he favored the rich people. He thought the country should be ruled by a few men who were wealthy and who had good educations. He believed that the common people could not be trusted to rule themselves.

Jefferson believed that the federal government should have very little power. He thought that most of the power should belong to the states. Hamilton believed in a strong federal government.

Hamilton wanted to see many factories in the United States. Jefferson wanted the United States to be a nation of farmers.

Some people thought Jefferson was right; others thought Hamilton was right. Those who followed Hamilton were called Federalists. Those who followed Jefferson were called Democratic-Republicans. These were the first political parties in the United States. There have been two political parties almost all the time since then. Today, the two parties are the Republican Party and the Democratic Party.

President Washington did not belong to either political party. However, he sided with the Federalists more often than he did with the Democratic-Republicans.

When you look at the United States today, whose ideas do you think have won out, Hamilton's or Jefferson's?

In some matters, Hamilton's ideas are followed. In other ways, Jefferson's ideas have won. The United States has become a government of the people, as Jefferson wished. Almost every man and woman over twenty-one may vote. Hamilton would not have liked this. In his day only a few men had the privilege of voting.

But the federal government has become much stronger than Jefferson would have wished. This would have made Hamilton happy. The United States has many factories today. More people make their living in factories than on the farms. Hamilton would have liked this, and Jefferson would not.

Even though Jefferson and Hamilton did not agree, both were good, honest, able men. Both were good Americans and loved their country. Both served their country well.

Washington's Second Term. After four years, Washington's first term was over. He wanted to go home to Mount Vernon, Virginia, but the people would not hear of it. They elected him President again.

The second time that Washington took his oath of office as President he did so in Philadelphia. Philadelphia had become the capital of the United States by act of Congress.

The City of Washington. Many people were not satisfied with New York or Philadelphia as the capital of the United States. They said the government should have a city of its own.

A beautiful piece of land on the Potomac River was chosen for the capital city. Virginia and Maryland each gave part of the land needed for the city. The land became known as the District of Columbia. The District of Columbia is not part of any state. It belongs to the federal government.

What should the new city be called? George Washington suggested that it be called Federal City. But most people thought it should be named in honor of the "Father of Our Country."

A great French engineer planned the new city. When he drew the first plans, there was nothing but a wilderness where the capital city now stands. Today, Washington is one of the most beautiful cities in the world.

George Washington laid the cornerstone of the Capitol in 1793.

You have just read two words that are much alike, capital and Capitol. "Capital" means the city in which the government is carried on. "Capitol" means the building in which the laws are made.

The Death of Washington. When Washington's second term was over many people begged him to become President for a third time. This time he said, "No." He said that two terms were enough for a President.

Washington went back to his beloved home, Mount Vernon, in Virginia. He died two and a half years later.

All Americans were sad when they heard about the death of this great American, the man who was "first in war, first in peace, and first in the hearts of his countrymen."

President John Adams. When Washington's second term ended, John Adams of Massachusetts was elected President. He had already served his country well for many years. He had been a member of the First Continental Congress, and had favored the Declaration of Independence. After the Revolution Congress had sent Adams to England to help make the treaty of peace. He was the Vice-President during Washington's two terms of office.

Although he was capable, Adams was never popular. As President he should be remembered for keeping us out of war with France.

STUDY LESSON

WHERE IS IT? Answer each question in a complete sentence.

1. In what city did Washington take the oath of office as President for the first time? the second time?
2. From what state did the first Attorney General come?
3. Washington, D. C., is on land which once belonged to which states? On what river is the city located?

WHAT IS IT? Write each word or name and after it the phrase that explains it.

1. Capitol
2. Attorney General
3. cabinet
4. Secretary of State
5. Democratic-Republican
6. Federalist
7. capital

a. the political party which tried to keep the control of the government in the hands of a few people
b. the building in which the laws are made
c. the party that tried to give control of the government to the people
d. the city where the government is carried on
e. the lawyer for the government
f. the man who takes care of our country's business with foreign governments
g. the group of men who help the President

WHO AM I? Write each name and after it the phrase that tells about him.

1. John Adams
2. Alexander Hamilton
3. George Washington
4. Edmund Randolph
5. Henry Knox

a. the Virginia lawyer who became our first Attorney General
b. the first man who took charge of our army and navy
c. the man who was "first in war, first in peace, and first in the hearts of his countrymen"
d. Washington's Secretary of the Treasury
e. the second President of the United States

WORDS TO KNOW. Use each of these words in a sentence. Look them up in your dictionary if you are not sure of their meaning.

attorney   treasury
staff   political party

SOMETHING TO THINK ABOUT. Think carefully before you answer these questions.

1. Why did George Washington refuse a third term as President?
2. Why did Hamilton have a hard job as first Secretary of the Treasury?
3. What did Hamilton believe? What did Jefferson believe?

192

21. Thomas Jefferson and His Friends

Jefferson, the Third President. The man in the picture is Thomas Jefferson. He has just left his boardinghouse in Washington. He is on his way to the Capitol. There he will take his oath of office as President of the United States. It is March 4, 1801.

When Jefferson took his oath of office, he became the third President of the United States. Jefferson was the first President to take his oath of office in the new city of Washington.

Jefferson's Early Life. What kind of man was this new President, Thomas Jefferson?

Thomas Jefferson was born on a large farm in Virginia. As a boy he learned to love books, and he loved them all his life. He also learned to play the violin. He went to William and Mary College, which was in Williamsburg, Virginia. This city was the capital of Virginia. The Virginia legislature, or House of Burgesses, met in Williamsburg. During his college days Thomas Jefferson often went to the House of Burgesses and listened to the speeches. Later he listened with great joy when Patrick Henry spoke in defiance of the English King.

Like George Washington, Thomas Jefferson had a big farm to look after. This could have kept him busy all his life. But he believed he had a duty to his country. He gave almost his whole life to serving his country.

Soon after he left college, Jefferson became a member of the House of Burgesses. Next he became a member of the Continental Congress. As we know, he wrote the Declaration of Independence while he was a member of this Congress. This was one of the most important works of his life.

During the last part of the Revolution, Jefferson was the governor of Virginia. Once, while he was governor, he was almost captured by the British. He was warned that the British were coming and he escaped just in time.

After the Revolution, Jefferson was the United States Minister to France. We know from the last chapter that he was Secretary of State when George Washington was President. He was Vice-President while John Adams was President.

In 1800 Thomas Jefferson was elected President. As we have just read, he took the oath of office as President on March 4, 1801.

All his life Jefferson worked for freedom and democracy. "Democracy" means rule by the people. Jefferson believed that the people should be allowed to rule themselves. He also believed that the people should be allowed to say what they think, read what they please, and worship God in the way that seems right to them.

That is why Jefferson wrote in the Declaration of Independence that all men are created free and equal. He also wrote that we all have the right to life, liberty, and the pursuit of happiness.

Farm Goods Were Floated Down the Mississippi River. On page 196 you can see how big the United States was when Jefferson became President. The United States owned the land from the Atlantic Ocean to the Mississippi River. Most of the people lived near the Atlantic Ocean. The thirteen original states were along the Atlantic coast.

Hundreds of families were moving across the Appalachian Mountains. Between the Appalachians and the Mississippi River these people found plenty of free land. They cleared the forests and started farms. They raised corn, wheat, cattle, and hogs.

They raised more of these things than they could use. How could they sell what they did not use? This was a big problem. There were no roads over the Appalachian Mountains. There were no railroads. The farmers found that the best way to transport their produce was to put it on flatboats and float it down the Ohio River to the Mississippi River. Then they would float the boats down the Mississippi River to New Orleans. At New Orleans the farm products could be put on ships. From there they could be taken either to the eastern part of the United States or to Europe.

There was one great difficulty with this plan: New Orleans did not belong to the United States. New Orleans belonged to France. **As the map on page 196 shows,** France owned New Orleans and also a vast stretch of land called Louisiana which was west of the Mississippi River.

Suppose France should say that the Americans could no longer use the city of New Orleans. Then thousands of farmers would no longer be able to sell their products. They would have no money. They would probably lose their farms as well.

President Jefferson did not want such a thing to happen. He sent two men to France to see if they could buy New Orleans.

The United States Buys Louisiana. Napoleon Bonaparte was then the ruler of France. Napoleon surprised the two men whom Jefferson sent to France. He offered to sell not only New Orleans but the whole territory of Louisiana.

The Americans accepted Napoleon's offer. They paid $15,000,000 for Louisiana. This was the biggest piece of land ever sold.

What a bargain it was! The Louisiana Purchase almost doubled the size of our country. Now the United States stretched all the way to the Rocky Mountains instead of to the Mississippi River. Louisiana contained great and fertile plains. It had thousands of acres for farms and immense grazing land for cattle. In the mountains gold and silver and other metals were waiting for the miners.

Fifteen states, in whole or in part, have been formed from the Louisiana Territory.

The Louisiana Purchase was made in 1803. It was one of the most important things that happened while Jefferson was President. It meant that the United States could keep on growing and would become a large country.

The Lewis and Clark Expedition. President Jefferson wanted to know more about the land he had bought from France. Congress gave the money, and a party of explorers was formed. The two leaders of the exploring party were Captain Merriwether Lewis and William Clark. William Clark was a younger brother of George Rogers Clark, the hero of the Revolution.

The Lewis and Clark expedition started out from St. Louis. At that time St. Louis was a small fur-trading post on the Mississippi River.

The party began its long journey in the summer of 1803. There were forty-five men in three boats. Up the Mississippi they went till they came to the mouth of the Missouri River. Then they started up the "Big Muddy," as the Missouri River was called.

It was hard work to make the heavy boats go against the strong current. The river wound through great grassy plains. The men saw thousands of buffalo. By autumn, Lewis and Clark had reached what is now North Dakota. They stayed there for the winter.

Sacajawea, the Bird Woman. In Dakota the explorers met an Indian woman whose name was Sacajawea. Her name means Bird Woman. She had been born in the mountains to the west. She offered to help Lewis and Clark. When spring came, the party resumed their journey. This time the Bird Woman led the way.

The party had many adventures. After passing through the Louisiana Territory the party crossed the high Rocky Mountains. Here they had a hard time finding their way. Their food supplies were low. At length the explorers came to a great river. It was the Columbia River. Lewis and Clark had reached the Oregon country. Canoes were made by burning out logs. The party floated down the Columbia River in their clumsy canoes. Finally they came in view of the great Pacific Ocean.

The journey home was equally hard and dangerous. There were grizzly bears, rattlesnakes, insects, and unfriendly Indians. After more than two years Lewis and Clark again reached the Mississippi River. They had traveled eight thousand miles.

Lewis and Clark kept a journal of their trip. Every day they wrote a description of what they had seen. This diary told about the places they had visited. It described the lives of the Indians. It reported where minerals could be found. It told where fur-bearing animals could be hunted.

President Jefferson was happy with the results of the Lewis and Clark expedition. He saw what a bargain the United States had made when it bought the territory of Louisiana.

Zebulon Pike. Between 1805 and 1807, another group explored the western part of North America. This expedition was led by Lieutenant Zebulon Pike. Pike and his party went beyond the limits of the Louisiana Territory into Spain's territory in the West and Southwest. Pike reached what is now Colorado and discovered the snow-covered mountain we call Pike's Peak. He was arrested by Spanish soldiers, then freed. Later he wrote an account of his travels which helped make the West known to Americans.

Cushing

Portland, known as the City of Roses, is Oregon's leading city today (top). Snow-capped Mount Hood can be seen in the background. The city grew up in the wilderness explored by Lewis and Clark. A statue of the Bird Woman, Sacajawea, stands in Washington Park.

Grand Coulee Dam (bottom) is the world's greatest source of hydroelectric power. It is located on the Columbia River in the northeastern part of Washington. Completed in 1942 at a cost of many millions, this picture is far different from the wild scene viewed by Lewis and Clark.

Monkmeyer

American merchant ships in the Mediterranean Sea were being seized and held for ransom by the Moslem pirates of North Africa.

In 1801 President Jefferson sent Captain Decatur to stop the piracy. After several years of sea battles, the pirates asked for peace.

War Against the Pirates. Pirates from Tripoli and other little countries in North Africa were seizing merchant ships in the Mediterranean Sea. The pirates kept the ships and their cargoes. They sold the sailors as slaves. President Jefferson said that this would have to stop. In 1801, he sent several ships to the coast of Africa to make war on the pirates. The rulers of the North African states became frightened and asked for peace. That was the end of pirate attacks in the Mediterranean! Jefferson's actions helped not only the United States but also the countries of Europe.

Pope Pius VII said: "The Americans have done more for Christendom against the pirates of Africa than all the powers of Europe united."

Jefferson Tries to Avoid War. The United States won its little war against the pirates, but there was danger that our country would get into a bigger war. England and France were fighting a big war on both land and sea. The French stopped American ships that were sailing to England. The English stopped American ships that were sailing to France. The English did more than that. When they stopped the American ships, they took off any sailors who had been born in England. They needed every man they could get for their war with France. They said, "Once an Englishman, always an Englishman."

Many Americans were becoming angry at both the French and the English. "They are ruining our shipping," Americans said. "And the English have no right to take sailors off American ships. We may have to go to war to stop this."

But President Jefferson did not want war with France or England. The United States was a young country and not very strong. Jefferson was afraid the country would be ruined by war. Jefferson did everything he could to prevent war. He asked Congress to pass a law saying that no ships could enter or leave American harbors. This was called the Embargo Act.

Shipowners and merchants did not like the Embargo Act. "It is ruining our business," they said. "Our ships are lying idle when they should be sailing the seven seas. We are losing money, and hundreds of men are out of work."

Later Congress said that Americans could not trade with France or England, but they could trade with other countries. Shipowners and merchants said that this law was a little better, but they were still not happy.

Until this time there had been few factories in the United States. Americans had been buying their manufactured goods from Europe. With the new laws, there was no longer so much trade with Europe. Americans had to manufacture their own goods. Many new factories were built in our country. The United States was becoming a manufacturing nation.

Hamilton's Death. Although Hamilton and Jefferson belonged to different political parties, Hamilton worked to get Jefferson elected President in 1800. Hamilton did this because he trusted Jefferson, even though he did not agree with him. He distrusted the other candidate, Aaron Burr. A few years later Burr tried to bring New York into a union of states outside the United States, in return for the promise of the Presidency. Hamilton again interfered and Burr forced him to a duel. Hamilton was killed.

Madison and Monroe, the Fourth and Fifth Presidents. Thomas Jefferson, like George Washington, could have been elected President a third time. Like Washington, he refused a third term. The next President was James Madison, who was elected for two terms. After Madison came James Monroe, who was also elected for two terms. Both Madison and Monroe lived in Virginia, not far from Jefferson's home. They were both friends of Jefferson's, and they both went to him for advice.

The terrible war in Europe continued after Madison became President. Both sides harmed us. Americans were becoming more and more angry. But we could not fight both England and France. Which nation would we fight?

Congress Declares War Against England. Many Americans felt that England was hurting us more than France because England was taking sailors off our ships. Many Americans also thought that England was trying to get the Indians to attack our settlements in the West.

There was also a selfish reason why the United States chose to fight England. Canada belonged to England, and many Americans thought we could easily capture Canada and add it to the United States. There was a band of young men in Congress who wanted war. They were called the "War Hawks." These men had their way. In 1812 Congress declared war against England.

203

The War of 1812. The Americans found that it was not easy to capture Canada. They were driven out every time they tried.

If the Americans could not capture British territory, the British could not hold American territory for long either. The British captured the city of Washington, but they were forced to leave. They set fire to the city before they left.

After the British left Washington they tried to capture Baltimore. All night the British ships fired their cannon at the forts protecting Baltimore. There was a young American on one of the British ships. He had come to see about exchanging prisoners. His name was Francis Scott Key. All night he watched the bombardment. He wondered if the forts would be able to hold out until morning. Would the American flag still be flying? As he watched, Key put his thoughts into words. These are the words of "The Star-Spangled Banner," which later became our national anthem. When morning came, "our flag was still there." The British could not take the fort. They sailed away.

Battle of Lake Erie. One very important battle was fought on Lake Erie. Whichever side could hold Lake Erie would hold the West. Young Oliver Hazard Perry of the American Navy was sent to take Lake Erie. His men cut down trees and made their own ships. Then they sailed out to meet the British ships. The British fought hard, and Perry's ship started to sink. He rowed to another vessel. After a bitter battle, the Americans won a complete victory. The British fleet was captured. The West was saved for America.

The Americans fought well at sea. One American captain, James Lawrence, was wounded in a battle at sea. As he lay dying, he said, "Don't give up the ship." These words became the motto of the American Navy.

Battle of New Orleans. The one great American victory on land took place at New Orleans. Here, Andrew Jackson and his backwoodsmen defeated a fine British army. The battle was fought after the treaty of peace had been signed. The men who fought in the battle did not know the treaty had been signed because news travelled slowly in those days.

The treaty of peace was signed on Christmas Eve, 1814. It was a strange treaty because it did not mention the causes of the war. However, England had stopped taking our sailors. Since the War of 1812 the United States and England have been on friendly terms.

THE MONROE DOCTRINE

For 300 years Spain had ruled most of the lands south of the United States. She ruled Mexico, Central America, and all of South America except Brazil.

About 1820 most of the Spanish colonies won their freedom from Spain. They became independent countries.

PRESIDENT JAMES MONROE

President Monroe heard that several countries in Europe were planning to conquer the former Spanish colonies. He did not like this. He thought the countries of North America and South America should keep their freedom. Also, he did not wish the European countries to have colonies in our part of the world. In December, 1823, President Monroe read an important message to Congress. He said:

1 Nations of Europe must not try to conquer independent countries in America.

2 Nations of Europe could keep the colonies they had in America, but they must not try to add new ones.

3 The United States would not interfere in European affairs.

These ideas became known as the Monroe Doctrine. The United States has been guided by the Monroe Doctrine ever since President Monroe spoke his famous words in 1823.

Our Sixth President. After President Monroe came John Quincy Adams, who was Secretary of State under Monroe. He was the son of our second President, John Adams. John Quincy Adams was President from 1824 to 1828.

He was not a very popular President. He signed a bill putting a high tax on goods coming into this country. It caused both the North and the South to oppose him.

STUDY LESSON

WHERE IS IT? Write the name of each place and after it the words describing it below.

1. Washington, D. C.
2. Williamsburg
3. Virginia
4. France
5. New Orleans
6. Louisiana
7. St. Louis
8. "Big Muddy"
9. Tripoli
10. Lake Erie

a. the Missouri River
b. in 1803, a small fur-trading post on the Mississippi River
c. body of water on which a famous battle of the War of 1812 was fought
d. location of the House of Burgesses and the College of William and Mary
e. French city at the mouth of the Mississippi River
f. new city where Thomas Jefferson took his oath of office as the third President
g. North African country which was the base of pirates who seized our merchant ships
h. where Jefferson was once Governor and where he and Madison lived
i. country that owned Louisiana before 1803
j. vast lands bought by Jefferson from Napoleon for $15,000,000

WORDS TO KNOW. Use each of these words in a sentence. Look them up in your dictionary if you are not sure of their meaning.

legislature   duel
democracy   minister
embargo   journal
candidate   doctrine

207

WHAT IS IT? Write each word or name and after it the phrase that explains it.

1. House of Burgesses
2. democracy
3. Louisiana
4. Embargo Act
5. Monroe Doctrine

a. land west of the Mississippi River which was owned by France
b. rule of the people
c. a message to Congress which warned European nations not to try to conquer independent countries in America or start new colonies
d. law-making body in Virginia
e. law saying that no ships could enter or leave the United States

WHO AM I? Write each name and after it the phrase that tells about the person.

1. Francis Scott Key
2. Zebulon Pike
3. Napoleon Bonaparte
4. William Clark
5. Aaron Burr
6. Sacajawea
7. James Monroe
8. Andrew Jackson
9. James Lawrence
10. Oliver H. Perry

a. the ruler of France who sold us Louisiana
b. the Indian woman who helped Lewis and Clark
c. a man who discovered a mountain which has been named after him
d. the man who wrote our national anthem
e. a candidate for the Presidency whom Hamilton did not trust
f. the brother of a hero of the Revolution who went with Lewis to explore the Louisiana Territory
g. the soldier who won the Battle of New Orleans after the War of 1812 was over
h. the President who issued a warning to foreign countries to keep out of the Americas
i. the naval hero who gave our navy its motto: "Don't Give Up the Ship!"
j. the naval hero who saved the West for America in the War of 1812

SOMETHING TO THINK ABOUT. Think carefully before you answer these questions.

1. Why did Jefferson write in the Declaration that all men are created equal?
2. Why were we so eager to buy New Orleans?
3. How many states were formed from the Louisiana Purchase?
4. What were two of the causes of the War of 1812?
5. What did the journal of Lewis and Clark tell about?
6. Why was the Battle of Lake Erie important?

22. Andrew Jackson, a Man of the People

Jackson From the Backwoods. The first six Presidents of the United States came from the original states of Virginia and Massachusetts. They came from comfortable homes. George Washington, for example, owned a beautiful estate in Virginia. So did Thomas Jefferson. The first Presidents also had good educations. Most of them went to college.

In this chapter we are going to read about the man who became the seventh President of the United States. His name was Andrew Jackson. Jackson was different from the first six Presidents. He was born near the western border of South Carolina. At that time, this was rough backwoods country. His family was very poor. He did not have much chance to go to school.

Andrew Jackson's father and mother came from Ireland. They settled in the backwoods country. Andrew was born there in 1767. His father died, and Andrew was raised without knowing a father's care.

Life in the backwoods was rough and difficult. The people lived in rude log cabins. Their farms were very poor. There were few books and no newspapers. Many people could not read or write. There were few schools.

The Jacksons were even poorer than most of the people who lived in the region. In the forest there were birds and animals of many kinds. Andrew and his brothers often went hunting and brought home the animals they shot or trapped. In the picture we see Andrew bringing home a deer. The Jacksons used

209

deer meat for food. They used deerskin for clothing. The neighbors were very kind to the Jacksons. They helped the Jacksons to get food and clothing, and they found little jobs for the Jackson boys.

Captured by the British. During the Revolution, British soldiers overran the country where the Jacksons lived. The three Jackson boys joined the American forces. Andrew was only thirteen years old at that time. Andrew's brother, Hugh, died in the fighting. Andrew and his other brother, Robert, were captured by the British.

A British officer, according to one account, ordered Andrew to clean his muddy boots. Andrew refused. The officer became so angry that he raised his sword to strike the boy. Andrew saw the sword coming, and he raised his left hand. The sword hit his hand and his face. He had a scar on his face for the rest of his life.

Then the officer turned and hit Robert with the sword. Robert never recovered from the wound.

Mrs. Jackson went to the British commander and begged him to let her two sons go free. He did so. Both boys were very sick. Robert died soon after he reached home. It seemed that Andrew might die, too, but he finally recovered.

Mrs. Jackson then went to take care of some sick American soldiers. She herself became sick and died.

At fourteen, Andrew was left all alone in the world. His father, mother, and two brothers were all dead.

Jackson Becomes a Hero. Andrew Jackson learned to read and write. He made up his mind to become a lawyer. He studied hard. He moved to the town of Nashville, in Tennessee. There he did very well as a lawyer. He ran for public office and was elected to the United States House of Representatives when he was 29. He was elected to the United States Senate when he was 30. He was a judge of the Supreme Court of Tennessee when he was 31.

Jackson joined the army during the War of 1812. He was such a good soldier that he was made a general. He won a victory over the Creek Indians who were fighting on the side of the British. In 1815 he defeated the British in the Battle of New Orleans. This was the only great victory the Americans won on land. Andrew Jackson became a great hero to the American people.

Jackson Invades Florida. Andrew Jackson stayed in the army after the War of 1812. He had many exciting adventures.

JACKSON'S CAMPAIGNS AGAINST THE SEMINOLES

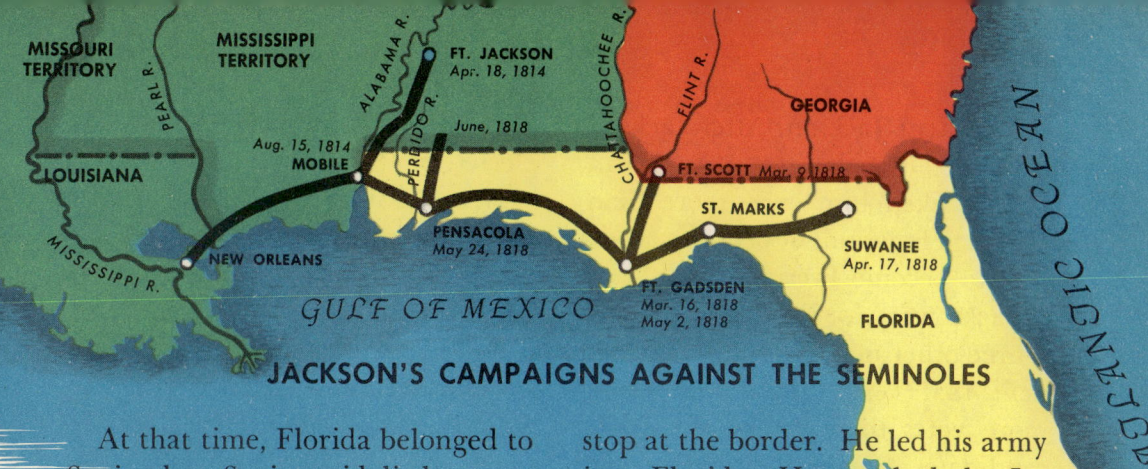

At that time, Florida belonged to Spain, but Spain paid little attention to the territory. Florida was filled with people who made trouble for the United States.

The Seminole Indians lived in Florida. The Seminoles often attacked settlements in Georgia. Then they dashed back into Florida before they could be captured.

Pirates and robbers also made Florida their hiding place.

General Andrew Jackson was told to go to the Florida border. He was supposed to keep the Indians and robbers from crossing the border into Georgia. But Jackson did not stop at the border. He led his army into Florida. He attacked the Indians and outlaws on their own ground. He hanged two men. Soon all Florida was under his control.

The Spaniards were furious when they heard what Jackson had done. They said he had no right to take an American army into Spanish territory.

A peaceful way was found to settle the matter. In 1819, the United States bought Florida from Spain for $5,000,000. Andrew Jackson became the first American military governor of the Territory of Florida a few years later.

President Jackson. After Jackson invaded Florida, the American people liked him even more than before. Thousands of people wanted him to become President.

Jackson ran for President in 1824. Three other men also ran for President that year. Jackson received more votes than any of the other candidates, but he did not receive enough to be elected. This meant that the House of Representatives had to choose the President. The House of Representatives chose John Quincy Adams.

Jackson's friends were furious. They said he really should have been President because he had received the most votes. His friends worked hard for the next four years to make Jackson President. He was elected in 1828.

Great crowds of people came to Washington to see Andrew Jackson take the oath of office on March 4, 1829. Some of these people came from hundreds of miles away. The people loved and admired Andrew Jackson. They felt that Jackson knew and understood them. They said that he was a "man of the people." After Jackson took the oath of office he made a short speech. Then he pushed his way through the huge crowds to the White House. Hundreds of his friends and admirers pushed their way into the White House. Jackson was in danger of being crushed. He finally had to slip out of the White House.

The "Spoils System." After Jackson became President he turned many men out of government jobs. In their places he appointed men who had worked to get him elected.

This was known as the "spoils system." It got its name from the slogan: "To the victor belong the spoils." The spoils, or rewards, were government jobs.

President Jackson was a good, patriotic American. He thought he was doing a good thing when he used the spoils system. He said that he had been elected by the people, and that he wanted to give the government jobs to the ordinary people.

We know now that the spoils system is a bad system. It is not fair to turn a man out of office just because his party has lost the election. Very often a man who is appointed simply because he helped win the election does poor work in that office.

South Carolina and the Tariff. While Jackson was President the state of South Carolina got into a dispute with the federal government. This dispute was about the tariff. A tariff is a tax which Congress places on goods brought into this country. For example, an American farmer who wished to buy tools from England would have to pay both the price of the tools and a tariff, or tax, to the United States government.

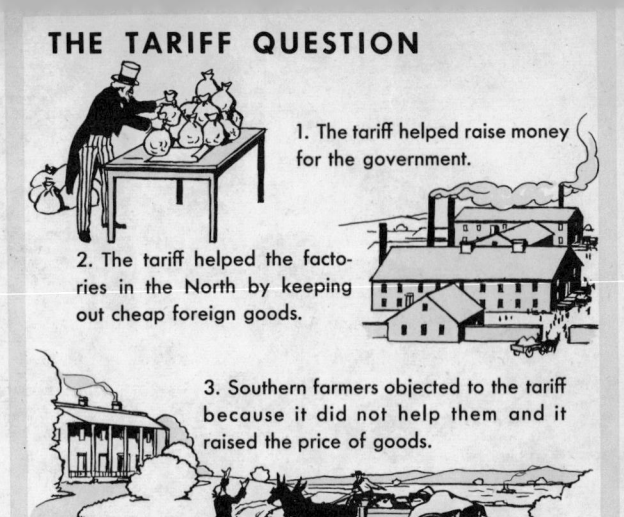

There are two reasons for a tariff.

The first reason is to get money to run the government.

The second reason is to help manufacturers in this country. Manufacturers said that without the tariff people would buy cheap goods from other countries. Our own factories would close and workers would be without jobs.

Manufacturers usually favor a high tariff, and farmers are usually against it.

The people of the South were farmers. They did not like the tariff. They had no factories. They wanted cheap clothes and cheap tools. The Southerners could see no reason why a farmer should be taxed to help a manufacturer.

THE TARIFF QUESTION

1. The tariff helped raise money for the government.

2. The tariff helped the factories in the North by keeping out cheap foreign goods.

3. Southern farmers objected to the tariff because it did not help them and it raised the price of goods.

The people of South Carolina were very angry about the tariff law. They said that no tax on foreign goods would be collected in the seaports of South Carolina. The legislature of South Carolina passed a law which said that the tariff law was nullified in South Carolina. This meant that the law was not in effect.

Did the legislature of South Carolina have the right to nullify a law passed by Congress?

"Of course, a state can nullify a federal law," said many Southerners. "The states are older than the federal government. The states gave the federal government its power. The states can take back that power any time they wish."

"No," said many other people.

"The states do not have power to set aside laws passed by Congress. If this happened there would be no union. New York might set aside one law, Virginia another, and so on. Soon we would have no federal government."

Jackson Protects the Union. Jackson was born and raised in the South. Would he side with his fellow Southerners? He soon showed how he felt. He was invited to a banquet and asked to give a toast. He arose and sternly proposed this toast: "Our Federal Union: it must and shall be preserved."

Soon after this, Jackson ordered two warships to the South Carolina coast. He also told the army to be ready to march.

Before there was any real trouble,

Congress passed a new tariff law. It lowered the tax, little by little. The Southerners were happier now, and they no longer talked of setting aside the tariff law.

The danger to the Union had passed for the time. Years later there was more trouble between the federal government and the Southern states, ending in the Civil War.

Jackson was elected for a second term in 1832. In 1836 his friend Martin Van Buren was elected President. Then Jackson went to his home near Nashville, Tennessee, and there he spent his last years.

STUDY LESSON

WHERE IS IT? Answer each question in a complete sentence.

1. Where was Andrew Jackson born?
2. In what city did Jackson practice law?
3. Into what foreign territory did Jackson lead his men?
4. Near what city did Jackson win a great victory over the British?

WHAT IS IT? Write each word and after it the phrase that describes it.

1. tariff
2. nullify
3. spoils system

a. to declare that a law is no longer in effect
b. way of rewarding party workers by giving them government jobs
c. a tax on goods brought into the country.

SOMETHING TO THINK ABOUT. Think carefully before you answer these questions.

1. How was President Jackson different from earlier Presidents?
2. How did Andrew Jackson win fame before he became President?
3. Why was the spoils system bad for our country?
4. How did President Jackson protect the Union?
5. Can you think of two reasons why tariff laws are sometimes passed?

Unit Six
OUR NATION GROWS

23. Pathfinders to the West

Boone Blazes a Trail. The first settlers in our country lived between the Atlantic Ocean and the Appalachian Mountains. In colonial days few people tried to cross these mountains. All of the thirteen original states were along the Atlantic coast.

One of the first Americans to cross the Appalachians was a young man named Daniel Boone. He crossed the mountains for the first time in 1767. He saw the land that we call Kentucky. Boone came back to his home in North Carolina with wonderful stories of what he had seen. He said that Kentucky was a land of forests, where there were numerous fur-bearing animals. The rivers were stocked with fish. The land was good for farming.

A man named Richard Henderson heard Daniel Boone's stories. He decided to start a settlement in Kentucky. He hired Boone to help him.

In the picture above we see how Daniel Boone led settlers into Kentucky. Boone went first and cut gashes in the tree trunks to mark the way. This was called blazing a trail.

Other men followed the marks that Boone had made. These men

cleared a path by cutting down the smaller trees and the bushes. This made a trail wide enough for the settlers to travel with their pack horses.

Boonesborough, Kentucky. Boone led his settlers through the Cumberland Gap in 1775. This was the year the American Revolution started and one year before the Declaration of Independence was signed. In April, 1775, Boone started his settlement. It was called Boonesborough. Today we spell it Boonesboro. There was only one other settlement in Kentucky at that time. That was Harrodsburg which had been founded the year before.

A third settlement was started in Kentucky in 1775. The people wondered what to call their little village. Then they heard about the Battle of Lexington which had just been fought.

"Let's name the settlement Lexington, in honor of the brave men who fought in the battle," someone suggested.

And that became the name of the third settlement.

As the map shows, Tennessee is close to Kentucky. The first settlements in Tennessee were made about the same time that Daniel Boone led his settlers into Kentucky.

Adventures With the Indians. Most Indians who lived in Kentucky did not like to have white men moving into their country. They sent war parties to destroy the white settlements. This occurred during the American Revolution. The British, it was believed, helped the Indians by giving them guns and ammunition.

One Sunday afternoon Boone's fourteen-year-old daughter, Jemima, drifted down the Kentucky River in a canoe. Two other girls were with her. They were captured and carried off by Shawnee Indians. Boone and his friends followed their trail. They crept up on the Indians. They fired from their hiding places. The Indians fled and the three girls were rescued.

Once Boone was captured by the Shawnees. Chief Blackfish took Boone to the Indian camp at Chillicothe, Ohio. He adopted Boone as a son. Boone cut his hair like an Indian and put on war paint like an Indian. He pretended that he liked being Blackfish's son. All the time he was looking for a way to escape.

He heard the warriors say that they were going to attack Boonesboro. His wife and children were in Boonesboro. His friends were there. He could wait no longer. He must warn the settlers. He slipped away and fled toward Kentucky. He crossed the flooded Ohio River in a canoe. He struggled into Boonesboro. He had traveled 160 miles in four days.

The people in Boonesboro were warned, and they were ready for the Indians. The Shawnees tried for nine days to capture the little log fort. Then they gave up and returned home.

Boone Moves Farther West. Daniel Boone loved the wilderness. He loved to go trapping and hunting.

More and more settlers moved into Kentucky. They cut down the trees. They killed the animals or frightened them away. Daniel Boone was no longer happy. He took his family and moved into a wild part of West Virginia. There he could trap and hunt once more.

Settlers moved into West Virginia, and once more Daniel Boone decided to move. He said that he needed elbow room. When he was sixty-five years old he took his family to Missouri. He died in Missouri when he was eighty-six years old. Years later the State of Kentucky brought his body back to the state he had helped found. A monument was built over the grave of the great trail blazer.

The Northwest Territory. Daniel Boone fought Indians on the south side of the Ohio River during the Revolution. At the same time George Rogers Clark fought Indians to the north of the Ohio River. We read about Clark in Chapter 18. It was probably because of Clark's conquest that Great Britain agreed to give the United States the Northwest Territory when the treaty of peace was signed.

After the Revolution many settlers came to the Northwest Territory. Some came through northern New York where the mountains are not so high. Some floated down the Ohio River on flatboats. Others came into Kentucky by Daniel Boone's Wilderness Road. Then they crossed the Ohio River into the Northwest Territory.

Five states have been formed from this territory. They are Ohio, Indiana, Illinois, Michigan, and Wisconsin.

Alabama and Mississippi Are Settled by Cotton Farmers. In 1793 a man named Eli Whitney invented a machine called the cotton gin. This made it easy to take the seeds out of cotton. Suddenly the Southern farmers found that they could make much money by raising cotton. But cotton will not grow in the northern part of the United

219

Map labels:
BRITISH TERRITORY
OREGON COUNTRY Occupied jointly by United States and Great Britain
MICHIGAN TERRITORY
MISSOURI TERRITORY
SPANISH TERRITORY
ARKANSAS TERRITORY
ILLINOIS 1818 | IND. 1816 | OHIO 1803 | PENN. 1787 | N.J. 1787 | MD. | DEL. 1787
W.VA. 1863 | VIRGINIA 1788
KENTUCKY 1792
TENNESSEE 1796 | NORTH CAROLINA 1789
MISS. 1817 | ALABAMA 1819 | GEORGIA 1788 | SOUTH CAROLINA 1788
LA. 1812
SPANISH CESSION 1819
NEW YORK 1788 | VT. 1791 | N.H. 1788 | MASS. | CONN. | R.I.
Pacific Ocean | Atlantic Ocean | Mississippi River

States. It will grow only in the South. The cotton farmers wanted to find more land for farms. They rushed into Alabama and Mississippi. They cut down the forests and started great cotton plantations.

Our Country Grows to the Mississippi River. When Daniel Boone led his settlers into Kentucky in 1775 there were very few white people living between the Appalachian Mountains and the Mississippi River. By the time he died in 1820 there were several hundred thousand people living in that region.

Daniel Boone lived long enough to see seven new states formed from the wilderness region between the Appalachian Mountains and the Mississippi River. Congress voted to include these states in the Union, and to add them to the original thirteen. Boone's own state of Kentucky was admitted into the Union in 1792. The others were Tennessee, 1796; Ohio, 1803; Indiana, 1816; Mississippi, 1817; Illinois, 1818; and Alabama, 1819. Michigan and Wisconsin came into the Union after Boone died.

The United States had grown to the Mississippi River. But this was only the beginning. The country would keep on growing until it reached all the way to the Pacific Ocean.

STUDY LESSON

WHERE IS IT? Answer each question in a complete sentence.

1. Where did most of the early settlers live?
2. What mountains did Daniel Boone have to cross?
3. What town did Boone and his family start?
4. What other settlement was there in Kentucky at that time?
5. Name the third Kentucky settlement.

WORDS TO KNOW. Use each of these words or expressions in a sentence. Look them up in your dictionary if you are not sure of their meaning.

    blazing a trail   cotton gin
      gap   ammunition
               flatboats

WHO AM I? Write each man's name and after it the phrase that tells something about him.

  1. Daniel Boone   2. Eli Whitney
      3. Richard Henderson

a. the man whose invention was important to Southern farmers
b. the man who decided to start a settlement in Kentucky
c. a famous trail blazer

SOMETHING TO THINK ABOUT. Think carefully before you answer these questions.

1. How did Boone happen to settle in Kentucky?
2. How was a new trail blazed?
3. How did Lexington get its name?
4. Name the seven states which were admitted to the Union during Boone's lifetime.
5. How did the cotton gin change the farms of the South?

24. Texas, the Lone-Star State

Texas—Vast, Empty Land. "New Land" was the motto of the American pioneers. They pushed farther and farther west, seeking land for new farms.

We read in the last chapter that there were settlements all the way to the Mississippi River by the time Daniel Boone died. But the pioneers did not stop at the Mississippi River. They crossed the river and pushed on into the vast territory of Louisiana. As you remember, the United States had bought this territory from France in 1803.

Soon there were five states along the west bank of the Mississippi River. The land near New Orleans became the state of Louisiana in 1812. The other four states were Missouri, 1821; Arkansas, 1836; Iowa, 1846; Minnesota, 1858.

Some of the American pioneers crossed Louisiana and came to the Texas country. Here they found a vast land with much fertile soil. Texas was the land of opportunity for farmers, ranchers, and cotton planters.

But the American pioneers found that it was no simple matter to settle in Texas. Texas did not belong to the United States. It was part of Mexico which belonged to Spain.

The picture at the top of the page shows what happened when American settlers tried to enter Texas. Spanish soldiers stopped them. The soldiers said that no foreigners were allowed in Texas. All people who were not from Spain or Mexico were considered foreigners.

For many years very few people lived in Texas. There were some Indians and a few Mexicans. Texas was a vast, empty land.

The Father of Texas. In 1820 Moses Austin, an American who had moved west, went to see the governor of Texas. The governor lived in the village of San Antonio. Moses Austin asked the governor for permission to bring 300 American families to Texas. At first the governor would not give his consent. Then Austin met an old friend who knew the governor very well. This friend promised to speak to the governor. The governor changed his mind and said that Moses could bring the 300 families to Texas.

Then Austin started back to his home in Missouri. The journey was a long, hard one. He had to swim icy creeks and rivers. He became ill and died soon after he reached Missouri.

Moses Austin had a son named Stephen. Stephen decided to carry out his father's plans. He took some settlers into Texas in 1822. Then he found out that Mexico no longer belonged to Spain. Mexico had broken away from Spain and was now an independent country. Would the new Mexican government allow the Americans to settle in Texas? Stephen Austin went to Mexico City to find out. This was a long journey of 1200 miles over high mountains and through dense forests.

The Mexican government gave Austin the permission he wished. He went back to Texas to build a settlement. It was named Austin in his honor.

Stephen Austin is called the "Father of Texas" because he brought the first American settlers into Texas.

Trouble in Texas. The leaders of the Mexican government decided that more settlers were needed in Texas. Not very many Mexicans were moving there. Mexico therefore invited more Americans to move into Texas. The Americans came in great numbers. By 1830 there were 20,000 Americans in Texas. Many of the Americans who had been cotton planters brought Negro slaves to work on their new plantations.

Soon there was trouble between the Americans in Texas and the Mexican government. The Texans complained that they did not know how much land they owned or whether they would be allowed to keep the land. They said that they had no voice in the government. In 1830, Mexico said there could be no more slaves in Texas. Many Texans did not like this. They said that they needed the slaves to take care of the cotton fields. Therefore they disobeyed the law and kept the slaves.

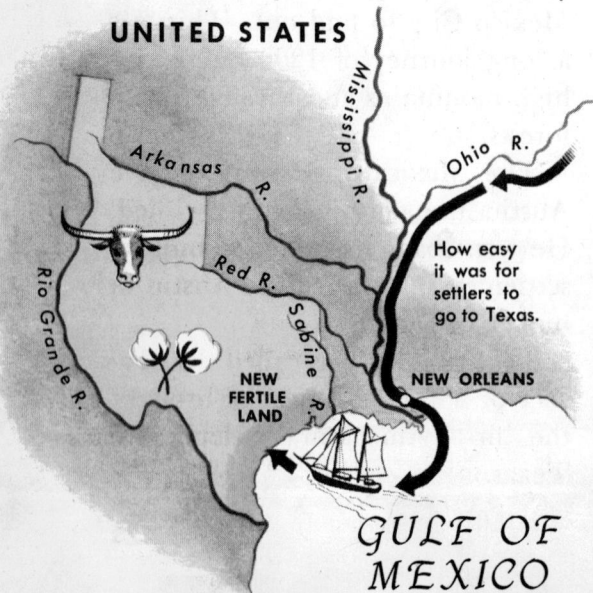

Because of all this trouble, the governor of Mexico declared in 1830 that no more Americans were welcome in Texas. The Americans did not pay any attention to this new law. They came to Texas in larger numbers than ever before. There were so many Americans pouring across the Texas border that the Mexican soldiers could not stop them.

In this dispute between the Texans and Mexico, the American Texans were at fault in some respects. Some Americans were looking for trouble when they moved into Texas. They were waiting for a chance to take Texas from Mexico.

On the other hand, the Texans were often treated very unjustly by the Mexicans. They had a right to complain about such treatment.

Stephen Austin worked hard to keep peace. He reminded the Americans that they were the guests of Mexico. He said they should behave as good guests.

Austin also asked Mexico to make Texas a state of Mexico. He asked Mexico to give the Texans a voice

How easy it was for settlers to go to Texas.

in their government. He said the Texans would be satisfied if they had more to say about their government. Then there would be no more trouble. Mexico refused to do this.

Texas Becomes Independent. A Mexican general named Santa Anna had become the ruler of Mexico. He called himself the President of Mexico. Actually he was a dictator. This means that his word was law. The people of Mexico had nothing to say about their government. They had to do as Santa Anna ordered them.

Santa Anna decided he would settle the trouble in Texas. He would show the Texans that they must obey him. In 1836 he marched into Texas with an army much larger than any force the Texans could muster.

In San Antonio the Texans had made an old mission into a fort. It was called the Alamo. Santa Anna attacked the Alamo and demanded its surrender. The Texans, led by Colonel Travis, refused to surrender, even though they were tired and hungry and their ammunition was low. There were only 188 defenders against several thousands attackers. Nevertheless, the Texans held out for eleven days. When Santa Anna finally took the Alamo, every single one of the defenders was dead.

Next Santa Anna attacked the Texans at Goliad. The Texans were again greatly outnumbered. They were forced to surrender. Instead of making them prisoners, Santa Anna had every one of them killed. All Texans were shocked and angry when they heard of this terrible massacre.

General Sam Houston had been made Commander-in-Chief of the Texans. He gathered together a force of 800 men. With this small force he attacked Santa Anna's much larger army. The battle took place at San Jacinto on April 21, 1836. The Texans rushed into the battle shouting "Remember the Alamo! Remember Goliad!" They defeated the Mexicans and took Santa Anna prisoner.

General Houston had been wounded in the battle. He was in great pain and was lying on the ground when Santa Anna was brought to him. Houston ordered Santa Anna to write an order saying that all Mexican troops should leave Texas. Santa Anna did so. The troops left, and Texas was free.

Texas was now an independent country. Its flag was red, white, and blue. It had one large star. Sam Houston was elected President of Texas.

Texas Joins the United States. Many Texans did not want Texas to remain an independent country. They wanted Texas to be one of the states of the United States. There were two reasons why they wished this:

1. Most Texans had come from the United States. They loved the United States and wanted to be part of it.

2. The Texans were afraid of Mexico. Mexico was a country of 7,000,000 people and there were only 50,000 people in Texas. But if Texas were part of the United States, the Texans would not have to fear Mexico.

In 1836 Texas asked to join the Union.

Not all Americans wanted Texas in the Union. Some Americans did not want Texas because it permitted slavery. Others were afraid we would get into a war with Mexico if we let Texas join the Union.

Congressmen talked about the problem for almost ten years. At last, in December, 1845, Texas was admitted as a state.

Texans are proud of their state and its fight for independence. They like to remember that they were once an independent country. They often hang their flag below the Stars and Stripes. They call their state the Lone-Star State, because of the one star on their state flag.

Our War With Mexico. Texas was now one of the states of the Union. But how big was Texas? The Texans said that their state went all the way to the river named the Rio Grande. Mexicans said that Texas went only so far as the Nueces River. They said that the land between the Nueces and the Rio Grande was part of Mexico. You can see the two rivers on the map.

The dispute about the boundary caused a war between the United States and Mexico. The war began in 1846 while James Polk was President of the United States.

General Zachary Taylor was sent with an American army against the Mexicans. "Old Rough and Ready," as Taylor was called, won the two great battles of Monterey and Buena Vista. Soon most of northern Mexico was in his hands.

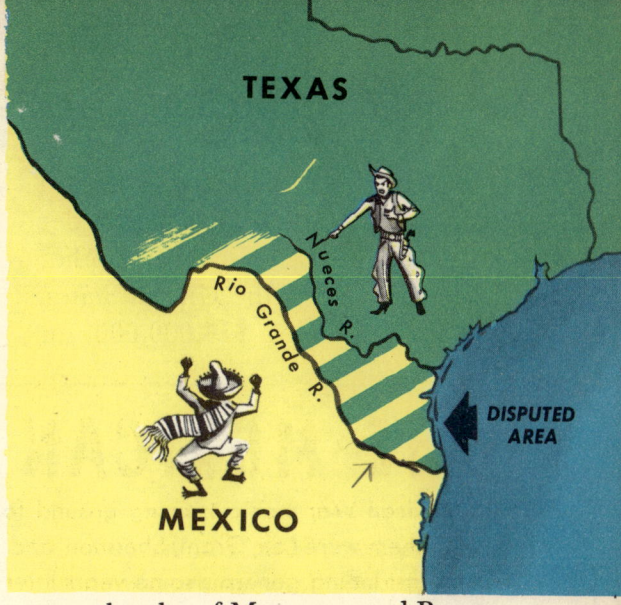

General Winfield Scott took an army to Vera Cruz by water. Then he marched across Mexico. He captured Mexico City, the capital.

The Mexicans were ready to give

up after their capital was captured. The treaty of peace was signed in 1848. In this treaty Mexico agreed that the Rio Grande was the border of Texas. Mexico also gave another huge territory to the United States. We paid Mexico $15,000,000 for this territory. The map shows the land that we gained from Mexico. The map shows how the United States was growing.

Our states of Texas, New Mexico, Arizona, Nevada, Utah, California, and parts of Colorado and Wyo-

THE MEXICAN WAR

The Mexican War was a training ground for young officers. Among them were Lee, Grant, Sherman, and Jackson, who became outstanding generals some years later in the Civil War.

GEN. A. L. DE SANTA ANNA
Mexican Commander-in-Chief

U. S. GRANT
later to lead the Union forces

R. E. LEE
later commander of the Confederate Armies

GEN. ZACHARY TAYLOR
"Old Rough and Ready"

GEN. WINFIELD SCOTT
"Old Fuss and Feathers"

W. T. SHERMAN
who was to fight well for the North

T. J. (Stonewall) JACKSON
who died for the South

THE STORMING OF CHAPULTEPEC

In order to capture Mexico City the Americans had to seize a very steep hill called Chapultepec. On top of the hill was an old fortified castle which was then being used as a boys' military school. Forty boys in their teens joined with Mexican soldiers in putting up a brave defense before the fortress fell.

ming have all been formed from land that once belonged to Mexico. After the Mexican War our country stretched across the continent from the Atlantic Ocean to the Pacific Ocean. Although we have acquired possessions and territories since then, our national boundaries are the same today as they were in 1853.

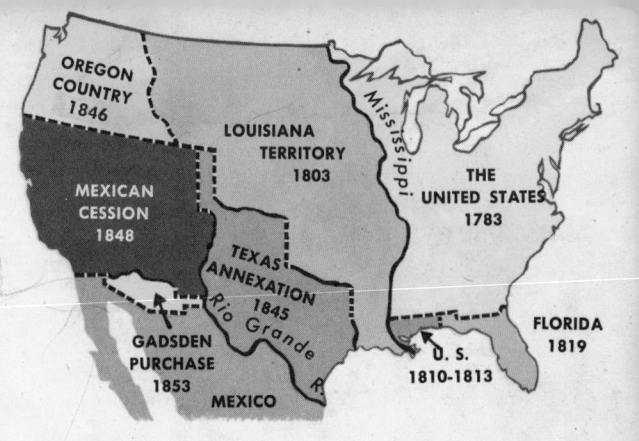

STUDY LESSON

WHERE IS IT? Answer each question in a complete sentence.

1. What five states were formed on the west side of the Mississippi River?
2. Name the states which were formed from land that once belonged to Mexico.
3. What is the southern boundary of Texas, the Nueces River or the Rio Grande?
4. Where was Austin's home?
5. What happened at San Jacinto?

WHO AM I? Write each man's name and after it the phrase which tells something about him.

1. Santa Anna
2. Stephen Austin
3. Winfield Scott
4. James Polk
5. Sam Houston
6. Zachary Taylor
7. Colonel Travis

a. the Commander-in-Chief of the Texans who took Santa Anna
b. brave Texan leader at the Alamo
c. the general who captured Mexico City
d. "Father of Texas"
e. the dictator who attacked the Alamo
f. "Old Rough and Ready" who won the battles of Buena Vista and Monterey
g. United States President during the Mexican War

WORDS TO KNOW. Use each of these words in a sentence. Look them up in your dictionary if you are not sure of their meaning.

pioneers   foreigners
dictator   massacre

SOMETHING TO THINK ABOUT. Think carefully before you answer these questions.

1. Who was right and who was wrong in the early dispute between Mexico and the Texans? Explain.
2. Why did the Texans want to be part of the United States?

25. California, the Golden State

The Spaniards in California. The priest in this picture is Father Junípero Serra. He is a Franciscan. The man with Father Serra is Captain Don Gaspar de Portolá. It is a hot day in July, in the year 1769.

Father Serra, Captain Portolá, and their men are arriving at the harbor of San Diego, in California. They have walked all the way from Mexico. It has been a long difficult march. It has been especially difficult for Father Serra who is very lame.

As you see in the picture, Father Serra and Captain Portolá find two ships waiting in the harbor. The ships have sailed from Mexico with food, tools, and clothes.

These men, on the shore of San Diego Bay, are the only white men in all California. But they are not the first white men who have seen California.

Juan Cabrillo discovered California in 1542, just fifty years after Columbus discovered America. Cabrillo was born in Portugal, but he was sailing for the King of Spain. He claimed California for Spain.

Some years later, Sir Francis Drake, the English pirate, reached California. He was on his way around the world. Drake claimed California for England.

In 1602 a Spanish sailor named Don Sebastian Viscaíno sailed along the coast of California. He discovered Monterey Bay and many other places.

For 166 years after that, nobody did anything about California. This was because there were many wars in Europe.

Mexico belonged to Spain at that time. About 1768 the Spaniards in Mexico heard that the English and Russians were planning to settle in California. The Spaniards decided to build forts and start missions in California before the English and Russians settled there.

That is why Captain Portolá and Father Serra arrived at San Diego in July, 1769. Father Serra was happy. For many years he had wanted to be a missionary to the Indians of California. Now, when he was 56 years old, he was getting his wish.

Father Serra's Missions. Captain Portolá left Father Serra at San Diego with a few men. Then he marched on to look for Monterey Bay. He marched past the bay without knowing it. One day while two of his men were chasing a deer they came to a great body of water. It was ocean water, but it was almost completely surrounded by land. They were the first white men to to see the great San Francisco Bay.

Meanwhile, back at San Diego, Father Serra's men built a little church. This was the beginning of the famous California missions.

Captain Portolá came back to San Diego. He was disappointed. He had not found Monterey Bay. Then Captain Portolá and Father Serra set out together. This time they went by ship and they found Monterey Bay. Captain Portolá started

231

his fort, and Father Serra opened his second mission.

"But two missions are not enough in this great land," said Father Serra. "There must be others with a good road leading from one to the other. All the Indians must hear of God. They must learn about the one true religion."

Father Serra sent letters back to Mexico. He asked for more priests, more soldiers, more food, and more tools. "Send bells, also," he wrote. "Bells must ring at each mission to call the people to Mass and to prayers."

Father Serra founded nine missions in California. They were a day's journey apart and Father Serra said they were like beads on his Rosary. The missions were connected by a little footpath called *El Camino Real*. These Spanish words mean The Main Highway.

A number of the missions founded by Father Serra are still in existence today, and many visitors to California go to see them.

Father Serra died in 1784, fifteen years after he had come to California.

After Father Serra died, other Franciscans arrived and founded more missions. Finally there were 21 missions serving the Indians in California.

Indian Life at a Mission. When the priests wished to build a mission they first built a simple little chapel, where Mass could be said. Then they built a small house for themselves. Next they hung some church bells, perhaps from the limb of a tree.

The Indians would hear the bells and would come to see what was making the noise. The priests would invite the Indians to come and live at the mission. At first the Indians were shy. They were afraid of the strange men in brown robes. Soon the Indians came to know and love

THE MAIN HIGHWAY

El Camino Real

- San Francisco Solano
- San Rafael Arcángel
- San José
- San Francisco de Asis
- Santa Clara
- Santa Cruz
- San Juan Bautista
- San Carlos
- La Soledad
- San Antonio de Padua
- San Miguel Arcángel
- San Luis Obispo
- La Purísima Concepción
- Santa Ynéz
- Santa Barbara
- San Buenaventura
- San Fernando Rey
- San Gabriel Arcángel
- San Juan Capistrano
- San Luis Rey
- San Diego

NEVADA

LOWER CALIFORNIA

the good priests. Then the Indians came to the mission quite willingly.

After a while the priests and Indians would start to build the real mission. The walls of the buildings were made of adobe. This is a kind of hard baked clay. The roofs were covered with red tile.

The principal building at each mission was the church. Near the church was a home for the priests and a hospital for the sick. There was a school, and there was a workroom where the Indians could learn simple trades. There were also buildings where the young Indians slept. Indians who were married had little homes of their own, close to the edge of the mission grounds.

Days at the mission were busy and happy. At sunrise the mission bells called the Indians from their homes. They went to church for morning prayers and Mass. Then they had breakfast. After that they went to work.

Some of the Indians worked on the farm. They raised wheat, barley, corn, and beans. Or perhaps they took care of the animals.

Other Indians learned a trade. Some of them were busy tanning hides, spinning, or weaving cloth. Some were carpenters. Others made wine, candles, or soap. The mission fathers trained the Indians to do a great number of useful things.

The Franciscan mission fathers brought to America fruits that had not been grown here before. From sunny Spain they brought oranges, lemons, grapes, and olives. These fruits are still grown in California. They help to make California a rich state.

On Sundays and holydays the Indians did not work. On other days they rested from eleven o'clock to two o'clock. This was the hottest part of the day.

The Indians at the missions lived happy, useful, Christian lives. This life continued until Mexico broke away from Spain. After that, greedy men took the mission lands. The missions fell into ruin and decay.

California Becomes American Territory. Father Serra went into California in 1769. He died in 1784. During this time, important things were happening on the other side of North America. The Declaration of Independence was signed, and the American Revolution was fought. A new nation was born—the United States of America.

The Americans who were fighting for their independence knew almost nothing about California. Father Serra and his missionaries knew very little about the United States. California and the United States were separated by many hundreds of miles. They were separated by forests, plains, deserts, and mountains. It was almost as if they were in different worlds.

As the United States grew, Americans moved farther and farther west. They moved to the Mississippi River and then across the Mississippi. They moved into Texas. The settlers were coming closer and closer to California.

A party of American fur trappers, led by Jedediah Smith, crossed the high Sierras into southern California. This was in 1826. By that time Mexico had broken away from Spain. California was part of Mexico. Smith and his followers found that some of the missions were still standing. He and his men were welcomed by the missionaries. Smith found that California had large ranches with huge herds of cattle. The ranches were owned by Mexicans. Most of the work was done by Indians.

Other Americans went to California. Soon there were more Americans than Mexicans in some parts of California.

An American army officer named John Frémont came into California. He had sixty men with him. Frémont and his men were seeking the shortest route to the Pacific Ocean.

In 1846, the Americans in California heard that the United States was at war with Mexico. They held a meeting and declared that California was free and independent of Mexico. Their flag was the famous Bear Flag——a piece of light cloth on which the figure of a bear was painted. The new government was called the Bear Flag Republic.

Meanwhile the American army and navy were getting to work. Commodore John Drake Sloat sailed into Monterey Bay with a small fleet of American ships. He raised the American flag over the Monterey Customs House. Later, Commodore R. F. Stockton took Commodore Sloat's place. He captured still more territory.

Colonel Stephen Kearney led some American soldiers into California. These soldiers defeated the Mexicans in several battles.

California became American territory at the end of the Mexican War in 1848.

The Gold Rush. California became part of our country in 1848. In that same year something very important happened in California. Gold was discovered. This is the way it happened:

John Sutter came to California from Switzerland. The Mexican government gave him a large tract of land. He was a good farmer and he raised large crops. With the money from the crops he bought more land. Soon he was one of the largest landowners in California.

Sutter hired a man named James Marshall to build a sawmill. The mill had to be run by water. Marshall dug a ditch to take the water to the mill. This kind of ditch is called a mill-race.

Marshall noticed some shining yellow grains in the sand of the mill-race. He picked them up. Could they be gold? He took them to Sutter. The two men tested the grains in every way they could think of. They were really gold!

The news spread all over America and even to Europe. "Gold has been discovered in California!" In 1849, men by the thousands left their work and started for California. The farmer left his crops. The rancher left his cattle. The storekeeper left his store. This was the California Gold Rush of 1849. The men who took part in it were called the '49ers.

There was no easy way to reach California from the East. Some people went across plains and mountains on horseback. Some traveled in covered wagons. Many of these people were killed by Indians. Others starved to death. Some died of thirst.

Some went to California by ship. There was no Panama Canal in those days, so these people had to sail all around South America.

Others went by ship to the Isthmus of Panama. Then they crossed the Isthmus on foot and took another ship to California.

When the ships reached California, even the sailors rushed off to the gold fields. There were hundreds of ships in San Francisco harbor with no one to sail them.

California Becomes a State. Many people died on the way to California, but many others reached there safely. Two years after gold was discovered, there were almost 100,000 people in California.

Many people who did not find gold found something better. They found a fertile soil and a delightful climate. They stayed and became farmers or ranchers.

By 1850 California had so many people that it was admitted to the Union as our thirty-first state.

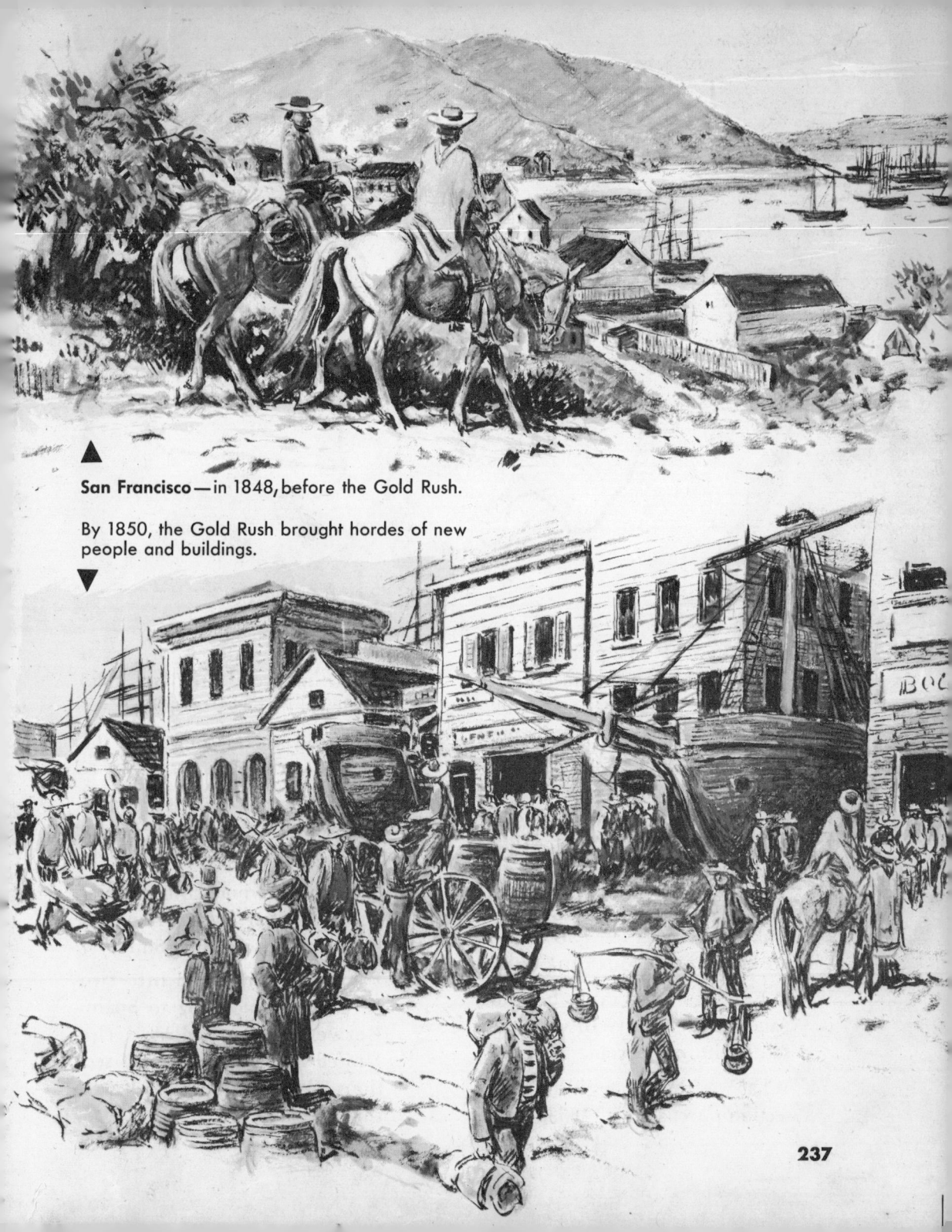

San Francisco—in 1848, before the Gold Rush.

By 1850, the Gold Rush brought hordes of new people and buildings.

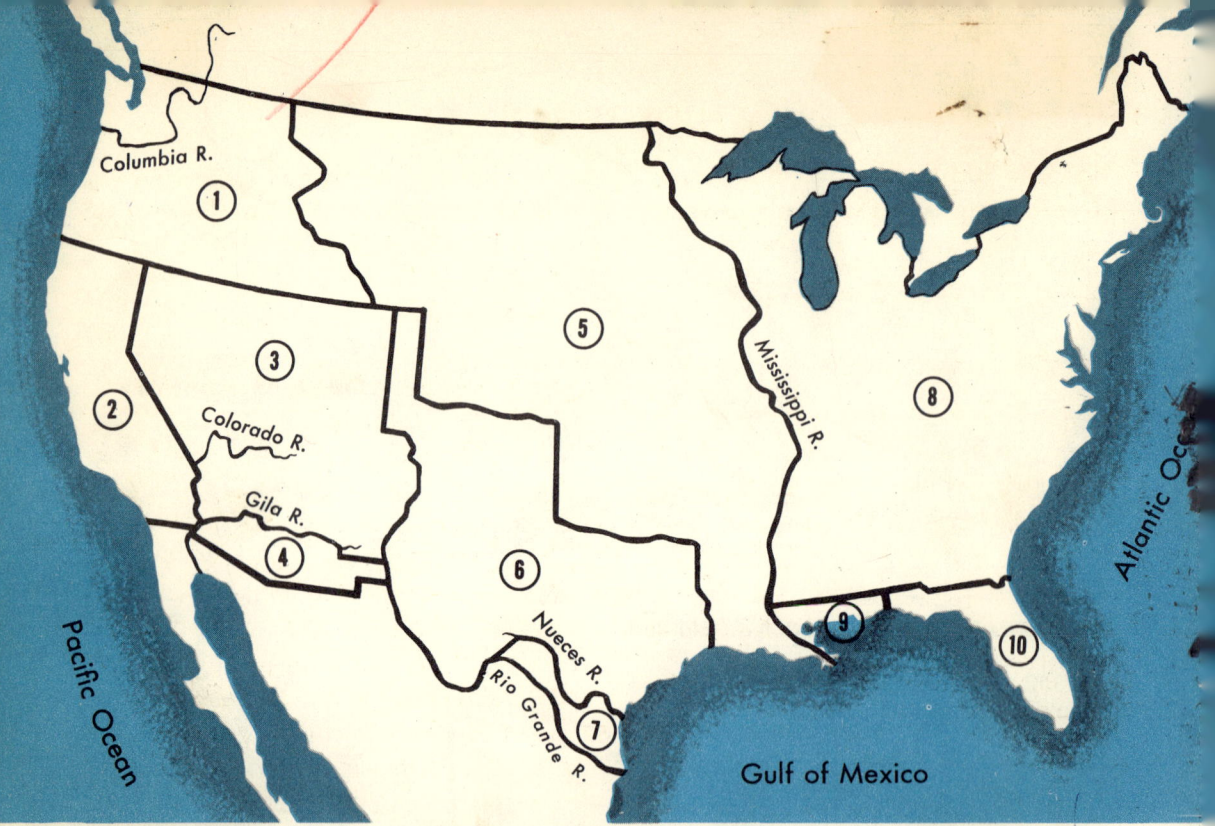

TRACE THIS MAP on a piece of drawing paper and crayon each section in a different color. Then make a key telling which states have been formed from each numbered section.

1. Which four countries claimed Oregon? How and when was the dispute between Great Britain and the United States finally settled?

2-3. Taken together these two sections are known as the Mexican Cession.

   When did this land become American territory? In what year did California become a state?

4. What was the name given to this section purchased in 1853?

5. How many states were carved from this great purchase? Who explored this vast territory?

6. How did Texas come into the Union?

7. The dispute about this area between what two rivers started the Mexican War?

8. This was the whole United States after what war? What river then formed the western boundary?

9-10. Florida was divided into two parts both belonging to Spain. Between 1819 and 1821 the United States bought both sections. Can you tell what led to this purchase?

STUDY LESSON

WHERE IS IT? Write each place and after it the phrase that explains it.

1. San Diego
2. El Camino Real
3. Monterey Bay
4. San Francisco

a. the early road from mission to mission, now a great highway
b. the city which grew up near the gold fields
c. where Father Serra built his first mission in California
d. the great harbor which Captain Portolá had trouble finding

WHO AM I? Write each man's name and after it the phrase that tells something about him.

1. Captain Portolá
2. Juan Cabrillo
3. Don Sebastian Vizcaíno
4. Sir Francis Drake
5. Father Serra
6. Jedediah Smith
7. John Frémont
8. John Sutter
9. James Marshall

a. the man who found gold in California while building a sawmill
b. the leader of a group of fur trappers who reached California in 1826 and were welcomed by the missionaries
c. the priest who started nine missions in California
d. the man who discovered California in 1542 and claimed it for Spain
e. a pirate who claimed California for England
f. the sailor who discovered Monterey Bay
g. an American army officer who led his men into California in search of the shortest route to the Pacific Ocean
h. a Swiss farmer and landowner on whose land gold was found
i. the leader of the first white men to see San Francisco Bay

WORDS TO KNOW. Use each of these words in a sentence. Look them up in your dictionary, unless you are sure of their meaning.

mission   isthmus
adobe   independence

SOMETHING TO THINK ABOUT. Think carefully before you answer these questions.

1. Why were Father Serra and Captain Portolá sent to California in 1769?
2. Why was Father Serra especially happy to go to California?
3. Why did the missionaries in California know little about the new nation, the United States?
4. What brought thousands of Americans to California the same year it became part of our country?

26. The Oregon Country

Americans Travel the Oregon Trail. The people in this picture are Americans on their way to Oregon. It is the year 1843.

Most Americans lived between the Atlantic Ocean and the Mississippi River in 1843. There were then only three states west of the Mississippi — Arkansas, Louisiana, and Missouri. Then Americans learned that there was a wonderful land called Oregon on the shore of the Pacific Ocean. They learned that the soil in Oregon was rich and that it would make good farm land. Many Americans decided to make their homes in Oregon. They traveled in covered wagons over the plains making a trail to Oregon. In time, this route became known as the Oregon Trail. It began at Independence, Missouri, and ended in Oregon. It was about 2,000 miles long.

Life on the Trail. It was too dangerous for just one family to start out by itself in a covered wagon, and so many families got together to form a wagon train. A captain was selected to head the party. A fur trader, or scout who knew the way, was chosen to guide the party over the trail. Many wagon trains traveled the Oregon Trail between 1843 and 1880.

Men, women, and children trav-

wagons, and were ready for another day on the Oregon Trail. On a good day, they would travel about 15 or 20 miles. They crossed wide prairies and high mountains. Sometimes there were rivers to cross. It took a wagon train five or six months to reach Oregon from Independence, Missouri.

The settlers were happy when they reached Oregon, but their work was just beginning. They still had to clear the forest, build houses, plow new fields, and plant crops All this was very hard work and it took a great deal of time. Only the hardiest people were able to cross the Oregon Trail and then settle down and make a living after they reached Oregon.

Dr. John McLoughlin. When the American settlers came to Fort Vancouver at the end of the Oregon Trail, they were greeted by Dr. John McLoughlin. Dr. McLoughlin was head of the Hudson's Bay Company in Oregon. He welcomed all settlers, and they were happy to see him after their 2,000-mile trip.

John McLoughlin was born in Canada in 1784. He became a doctor, but he did not practice as a doctor for very long. He loved the wilderness, and so he joined the Hudson's Bay Company. This was a fur-trading company with trading

eled in the wagon trains. Some rode in the wagons, and some rode on horseback. Large herds of cattle were driven along behind the wagon trains.

At night the wagons formed a circle. The men chained the wagons together. In this way, the wagons made a good fort. Sentinels were posted to watch for unfriendly Indians. Everyone else went to work. Children gathered wood and tended the fires. Women cooked the meals. Some of the men took care of the cattle. Others repaired the wagons. Still others went hunting, so there would be enough food.

Everyone went to sleep early, and everyone was up early. The settlers ate their breakfast, loaded their

241

posts throughout Canada. In 1824 the Hudson's Bay Company sent Dr. McLoughlin into Oregon. There were very few white men in Oregon at that time. It was a vast wilderness. It was a good place to get furs, because so many animals lived in the wilderness.

Dr. McLoughlin lived at Fort Vancouver on the Columbia River. When he came to Oregon, the Indians were very warlike. They fought each other, and they attacked white men who traveled through Oregon. Dr. McLoughlin made friends with the Indians. He told them it was wrong to fight. The Indians listened to him. They stopped fighting each other, and they stopped fighting the white men. It was said that a white man could travel by himself through the Oregon wilderness and never be attacked by Indians.

"The Father of Oregon." Indians and white trappers all brought their furs to Fort Vancouver. Dr. McLoughlin bought the furs and sent them back to the Hudson's Bay Company in Canada. Then the company would sell the furs for high prices in Canada, the United States, and Europe. For many years the company was happy with Dr. McLoughlin. He was doing his work well and making much money for the company.

When Dr. McLoughlin went to Oregon he was a member of the Church of England. He read about the Catholic Church and decided it was the One True Church. He became a Catholic in 1842.

Protestant and Catholic missionaries began coming to Oregon about 1843. Dr. McLoughlin welcomed them. In 1843 the first American settlers came in their wagon train. Dr. McLoughlin gave them food and clothes and took care of the sick. He gave them seeds to plant. He loaned them horses and plows. More American settlers arrived each year, and Dr. McLoughlin helped them all.

The new settlers hurt the fur trade. They cut down the forests. They killed the animals or frightened them away. When Dr. McLoughlin helped the settlers he was harming his own business. But that did not stop him. He knew that the settlers needed help, and so he continued to help them. In 1846, he lost his job with the Hudson's Bay Company. But he remained in Oregon, and he kept on helping the settlers.

Without Dr. McLoughlin's help, many American settlers would have had to leave Oregon. Because he had so much to do with settling this part of our country, John McLoughlin is called "the Father of Oregon."

Great Britain and the United States Both Claim Oregon. The map shows that the Oregon Country of 1843 was much bigger than our state of Oregon today. It stretched from the southern boundary of Alaska to the northern boundary of California.

At one time, four countries claimed Oregon. They were Russia, Spain, Great Britain, and the United States. Russia and Spain gave up their claims. This left only Great Britain and the United States. In 1818 the two countries agreed that they would own Oregon in partnership. This was called joint occupation. Dr. McLoughlin was a British citizen when he went there in 1824. He was born in Canada, and Canada belonged to Great Britain at that time.

THE APOSTLE OF THE ROCKIES

Father Peter De Smet, a Jesuit missionary, lived with the Indians of the Oregon Country from 1841 to 1873. He preached to them, taught them, and cared for them. He was the Indian's sincerest friend.

More and more Americans moved to Oregon. Most of them settled in the southern part. Very few British citizens settled there. The American settlers said that Oregon should belong to the United States. Many people in the United States also thought that Oregon should be American territory. They said they would not be satisfied with part of Oregon. They wanted all of it, up to the border of Alaska. The northern boundary, as the map shows, was 54 degrees and 40 minutes of latitude. The Americans who wanted all of Oregon shouted: "Fifty-four forty or fight." They were ready to go to war with Great Britain for Oregon.

Oregon Is Divided. For a time it looked as if there might be a war. The British said they would not give up Oregon. If they did, Canada would be cut off from the Pacific Ocean. Dr. McLoughlin worked hard to keep the peace. Although a British citizen himself, he advised the British government to give up the southern part of Oregon. He said that this part should go to the United States because so many Americans were living there. The British agreed to divide Oregon with the United States.

The Americans decided that they did not really want war, either. In 1846, the two countries agreed to divide Oregon at the 49th degree of

244

latitude. This was already the boundary between the United States and Canada farther east.

The British part of Oregon became known as British Columbia. Today, it is one of the ten provinces of Canada. The American part was known for a time as the Oregon Territory. In 1859 part of this territory was admitted to the Union as the State of Oregon. Later, two more states were carved from the territory. Washington became a state in 1889 and Idaho in 1890.

STUDY LESSON

WHERE IS IT? Answer each question in a complete sentence.

1. Where did most Americans live in 1843?
2. Where did the Oregon Trail begin?
3. At what fort did the Oregon Trail end?
4. What was the northern border of Oregon?
5. What was the southern border of Oregon?

WHAT IS IT? Write each name and after it the phrase that explains it.

1. Hudson's Bay Company
2. joint occupation
3. 54° 40′
4. 49th degree of latitude

a. point where Oregon was divided in 1846
b. fur-trading company with posts throughout Canada
c. America and Britain owning Oregon in partnership
d. old northern boundary of Oregon

WORDS TO KNOW. Use each of these words in a sentence. Look them up in your dictionary unless you are sure of their meaning.

wagon train   **wilderness**
prairie   **latitude**
joint occupation

SOMETHING TO THINK ABOUT. Think carefully before you answer these questions.

1. Why did the Oregon settlers travel by wagon train?
2. How long did it take to go from Missouri to Oregon?
3. Who was John McLoughlin? Explain his part in the settling of Oregon.
4. How did the new settlers in Oregon hurt the fur trade? Explain.
5. Why did England refuse to give up all of Oregon?
6. Do you think the final settlement of the Oregon question was a good one?

27. New Ways to Travel in a Growing Country

Most Early Travel Was by Water. In the early days of our country most people lived near the Atlantic Ocean. Ships from Europe sailed into the harbors along the coast. The first picture shows a ship that has just arrived from Europe. The people of the town are looking at the new hats, cloth, and kitchenware and other finished goods that have just arrived from Europe. They are reading newspapers and mail from Europe.

How do the people make the money to pay for the finished goods they receive from Europe? They earn it by selling raw goods to the people in Europe. When this ship goes back to Europe it will be loaded with raw goods from America. These raw goods include lumber, furs, dried fish, and farm products.

The second picture shows a family that lives back from the coast. The lives of these people are quite different from the lives of the people who live near the ocean. No ship can bring these people clothes, furniture, and other finished things from Europe. As the picture shows, the people have to make their own clothes and their own furniture. These people receive no news and no letters. They do not know what is going on in the rest of the world. They cannot sell the crops they raise on their farm, because there is no way to send these crops through the forest.

In time, all the land along the ocean was taken. More and more people settled back from the coast. These people wished to send their farm products to the cities on the coast and also to Europe. They wished to buy manufactured goods from the cities on the coast and from Europe. They also wished to know what was going on in the rest of the country and in the rest of the world.

If the United States was to be a strong country, ways had to be found to tie the country together. Ways had to be found to send goods across the country. Ways had to be found to send messages across the country.

Sending goods is called *transportation*. Sending messages is called *communication*. In this chapter we shall read how the American people solved the problems of transportation and communication.

The First Roads. The greatest need of the people who lived back from the coast was roads. With roads they could drive wagons or take their pack horses into the city with their crops, hides, and furs. They could drive back to their farms with goods bought in the city. With roads they could also receive mail and news.

It was not easy to build roads in the eastern part of our country. Almost all the land between the Atlantic Ocean and the Mississippi River was covered by one vast forest. In order to build a road, many trees had to be cut down. After the trees were cut the stumps had to be pulled out. Bridges had to be built over the rivers and streams. All this took a great deal of work and a great deal of money. The United States was a young country, and there was very little money.

247

The first roads were not paved. They were trails through the forest. These roads became very dusty in dry weather. In rainy weather the wagon wheels sank deep into the mud.

Someone thought of cutting down trees and putting the logs close together across the road. This kind of road was called a corduroy road because it reminded people of the cloth called corduroy. This cloth has many ridges, and the round logs made ridges in the road. The logs kept the wagon wheels from sinking, but riding on a corduroy road was rather rough.

Later on, better and smoother roads were built. Sand, gravel, and crushed stone were used to make hard, smooth roads. These roads cost more to build than the corduroy roads. People had to pay to use these roads.

Sometimes a traveller would be stopped at a gate blocking the road. This kind of gate was called a toll-gate. After the traveller paid the man at the tollgate, the gate was opened. Then the traveller could go on. The money which was collected at the tollgates was used to pay for the roads. The payments for the use of the roads were called "tolls."

The National Road. The most famous of the old roads was the Cumberland Road. This road was begun by the United States Government in 1811. It ran from Cumberland, Maryland, across the mountains to Wheeling, in what is now West Virginia. Later, the road was built westward to the Mississippi River. After being extended, it was known as the National Road. Stagecoaches carried passengers and mail over the National Road. Freight was carried in large canvas-covered wagons. These were called Conestoga wagons. Many pioneers, who were going west to settle, traveled as far as the Mississippi River on the National Road, which had been completed in 1818.

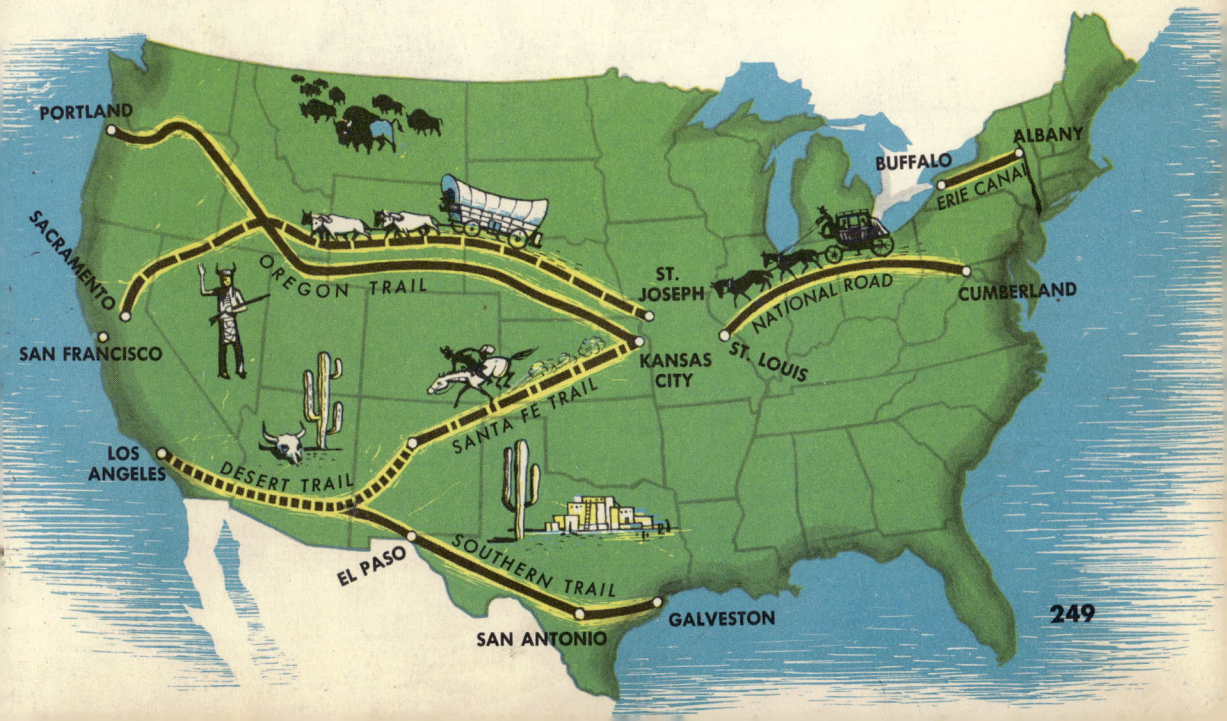

249

Farther west there were no real roads. Often the pioneers used trails made by the Indians and the buffalo. Buffalo trails were wide and deep and almost as practical as the rough pioneer roads. Two of the most famous trails were the Oregon Trail to the Northwest and the Santa Fe Trail to the Southwest.

To protect themselves against unfriendly Indians the pioneers often formed wagon trains. Added protection came from the forts which the army built along the trails. Cavalry troops stationed at these forts patrolled the wagon trails constantly. The settlers could stop and rest within the stockade surrounding each fort.

In its wagon each family of settlers carried clothes and furniture, seeds, tools, weapons, and enough food to last several months on the trail. Not long after they reached the end of their journey, the settlers began to need things. They found that many things had been forgotten, much had been lost or broken during Indian raids, and some supplies had been used up.

How happy they were the day the Yankee peddler arrived! His wagon was a store on wheels. Housewives flocked around him, eager to buy big bolts of cloth, needles, and thread. Among his wares, too, were tea kettles, pots, pans, brooms, butter churns, and harmonicas.

Most traders came from New England. They drove their wagons along the pioneer trails which had by this time been beaten into dirt roads.

Robert Fulton Builds a Steamboat. Robert Fulton was born in Pennsylvania ten years before the beginning of the American Revolution. When he was a young man he made a trip to England. Not many years before, an Englishman named James Watt had invented the steam engine. In England, Robert Fulton saw steam engines pumping water from mines and running machinery in factories.

Fulton had an idea. Why couldn't a steam engine be used to run a boat? Fulton went to Paris, France. There he met Robert Livingston, who represented our government in France. Fulton told Livingston about his plans for running a boat by steam instead of sails. Livingston was interested. He and Fulton formed a partnership. Livingston agreed to supply some of the money which Fulton needed to build his steamboat.

Fulton went back to the United States and built a steamboat. He named it the *Clermont,* which was the name of Livingston's estate on the Hudson. Many people called the boat "Fulton's Folly." They were sure it would never be able to move from the dock.

A large crowd gathered on the shore of the Hudson River one day in August, 1807. This was the day that the *Clermont* was to make its first trip. Fulton said it would go from New York to Albany, 150 miles up the river.

The signal was given, and the paddle wheels began to turn. The *Clermont* moved ahead. Then the wheels stopped. The crowd roared with laughter as the funny-looking boat tossed on the stream. The damage was repaired and once again the paddle wheels churned the water. Smoke poured from the tall stack. Sparks flew high in the air. Now and then there was a burst of flame. People thought the boat would blow up at any minute.

To their astonishment, the boat kept moving steadily up the stream. The people watched until it was out of sight. The *Clermont* continued up the river until it reached Albany. The trip took 32 hours. The ride back required only 30 hours.

Soon, the *Clermont* was making regular trips between New York and Albany. People were happy that they could now make the trip in less than a day and a half. To ride the same distance by stagecoach took about a week. Soon there were steamboats on all the large American rivers and on the Great Lakes. They made water travel much easier.

Steam engines were also put on sea-going ships. At first the ships used sails to help the engines. In 1838 the *Great Western* crossed the Atlantic Ocean using only steam. That was the first time that a ship had crossed the ocean without using sails.

The steamboat made it easier to travel between various parts of our country where there were waterways. The steamship made it easier to travel between our country and other parts of the world. The world now seemed a little smaller.

The "Big Ditch." The Mayor of New York City was De Witt Clinton. He had a great plan. He knew that many people were moving into the region around the Great Lakes. These people had many things to sell to the eastern part of the United States and to Europe. They had grain and other farm products, lumber, furs, and other raw goods. These people needed manufactured goods from the eastern part of the United States and from Europe. But transportation was the big problem. How could goods be sent to and from the region around the Great Lakes?

Roads were being built in some parts of the country, but it would be a long time before there were enough roads. Besides, it was more expensive to send goods by land than it was by water. Clinton's plan was to have an all-water route between the Great Lakes region and New York City. This could be done if there were a canal connecting Lake Erie with the Hudson River. Some said that it would be impossible to dig such a long canal. They laughed and called the plan "Clinton's Big Ditch."

Clinton went to Washington to see if he could get the federal government to supply the money for the canal. Federal officials told him that the State of New York would have to provide the money because the canal would be in that state.

Clinton was elected Governor of

New York. He persuaded the legislature to vote the money for the canal. Work started in 1818. The Erie Canal was completed in 1825. The main section of the canal cost more than $8,000,000. In those days this was a huge sum of money.

When the work was finished, Governor Clinton went to Buffalo, which was at the Lake Erie end of the canal. He boarded a gaily decorated canal boat. The boat was pulled by tow horses which walked along a towpath on the bank of the canal. People all along the way cheered the boat. At Albany, the boat left the Erie Canal and floated down the Hudson River to New York City. Here a cask of water taken from Lake Erie was poured into the Atlantic Ocean. This was called the "Marriage of the Waters."

New York City became America's largest and richest city partly because of the Erie Canal. The people of the West were helped because they were able to send their products all the way to New York City and on to Europe. Busy cities sprang up along the canal.

The Erie Canal has been improved many times. Today, it is called the New York State Barge Canal. A barge is a large flat-bottomed boat used for carrying freight on rivers and canals.

The Erie Canal was such a success that many other canals were dug in other parts of the country. The years between 1825 and 1840 are sometimes called the Canal Era. Beginning in 1828 many railroads were built and they took away much business from the canals.

THE RAILROAD STORY

Stagecoaches on rails were the first American railroads. The rails were made of wood with thin iron strips on top for easier riding.

An Englishman, John Stephenson, designed the first locomotive—a steam boiler and an engine on wheels. Americans soon began to build them.

The Rock Island steam train of 1852. This locomotive, a "wood-burner" with a large smokestack, is typical of those then in use. A later step in railroad development were the subways and elevated railways.

The locomotive *De Witt Clinton* had its first trial in 1831 between Albany and Schenectady, N. Y., a run of 17 miles.

Coal and oil replaced wood as a fuel for locomotives. The modern steam locomotive shown below is oil-driven. Electricity is also employed today to provide power.

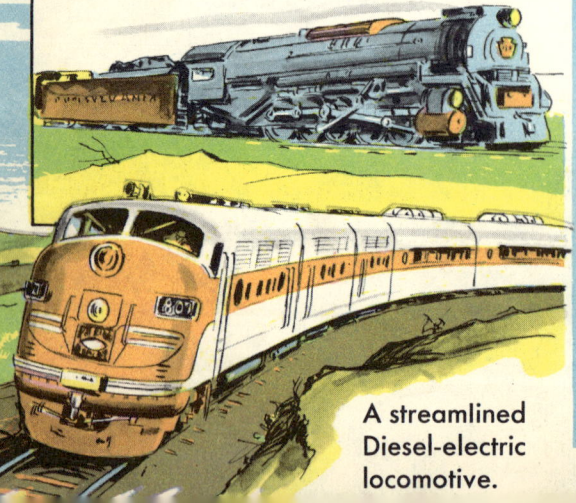

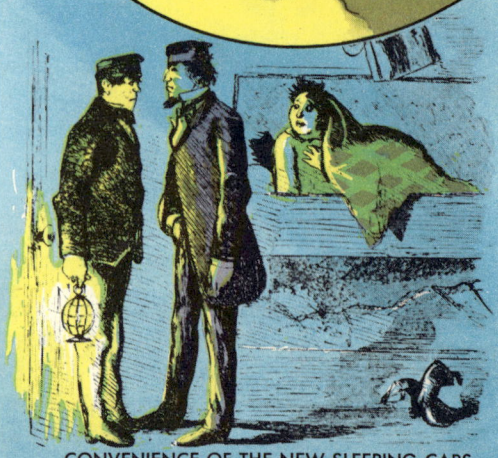

A streamlined Diesel-electric locomotive.

CONVENIENCE OF THE NEW SLEEPING CARS
(A timid old gent, who takes a berth in the sleeping car, listens.)
Brakeman: "Jim, do you think the Millcreek Bridge is safe tonight?"
Conductor: "If Joe cracks on the steam, I guess we'll get the engine and tender over all right. I'm going forward!"
(A cartoon from *Harper's Weekly*, May 28, 1859)

The Coming of the Iron Horse. After the Erie Canal was dug, some men in Baltimore saw that New York had become a very busy city.

"We should have trade with the West, too," thought these men. "But we cannot build a canal to the West. Here the mountains are too high. Instead we shall build a railroad over the mountains to the Ohio River."

That is how the Baltimore and Ohio Railroad came into being.

When the time came to begin building the railroad, a member of one of the oldest Catholic families in Maryland was invited to turn the first shovelful of earth. This was 1828 and Charles Carroll of Carrollton was now an old man of 91. He was the only man still alive who had signed the Declaration of Independence. Carroll knew that railroads would one day be very important in our country. As he took the shovel in his hand he said: "This act is the most important of my life, next to the signing of the Declaration of Independence."

The first cars on American railroads were usually old stagecoaches with wheels made to fit the rails. They were pulled by horses. The first rails were made of wood and had thin strips of iron nailed to the top.

The first steam locomotives used in this country were built in England. In 1830 an American named Peter Cooper built a steam locomotive. It was called the *Tom Thumb*. Soon, locomotives were pulling whole trains of cars, and horses were no longer used.

A trip on one of these old trains was interesting but not very comfortable. Passengers who could not pay very much rode on flatcars. They sat on rude pine benches. The richer people rode in coaches that were like stagecoaches. Smoke and soot from the locomotive often blew in the passengers' faces. The train reached a speed of about fifteen miles an hour. That seemed very fast in those days, and the passengers were often frightened by the speed.

After the Baltimore and Ohio, other railroad lines were built. These were usually short lines between near-by cities. By 1860 railroads reached from the Atlantic coast to the Mississippi River.

The railroad has probably done more than any other invention to make our country rich and powerful. It also made many changes in American life. With increased travelling and increased trade, people in the various sections of the country grew to know each other better.

Samuel Morse

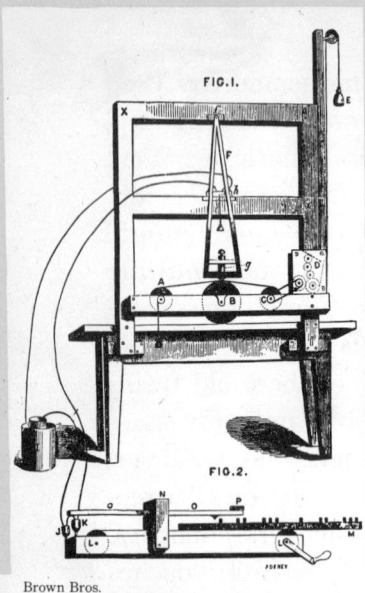

Left: diagram of Morse's telegraph equipment. *Right:* old Western Union telegraph set.

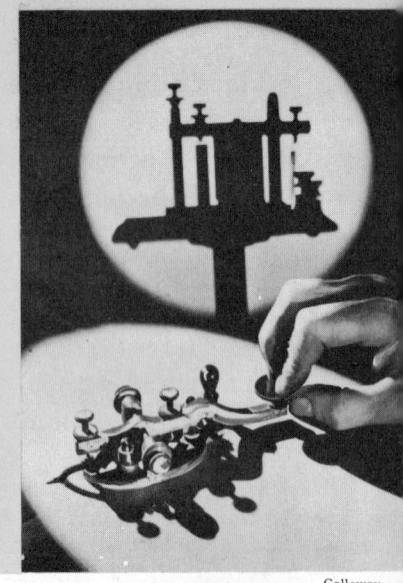

Morse Invents the Telegraph. Samuel Morse was born in Massachusetts in 1791. His father, a minister, was poor but he sent his son to college. Samuel was a good artist, and he helped pay his way through college by painting pictures. When he graduated, he went to London to study art. He knew that his mother would wonder whether he had arrived in London safely. He wrote to her: "I wish that in one instant I could tell you of my safe arrival, but we are 3,000 miles apart and must wait four long months to hear from each other."

Many other people besides Morse had wished for a quicker way to send messages. But it was Morse who finally solved the problem.

Morse had always liked science. He was interested in electricity. He knew that electricity could pass through a wire in an instant. He had an idea: Why could not messages in the form of signals be sent over the wire by stopping and starting the current?

By the time Morse was forty years old he was a successful artist, but he gave up his art to work on his idea for sending messages. In 1837 he made the first telegraph out of an old clock, scraps of wood and metal, and bits of wire.

This first telegraph sent a message over a short distance. Would it work over a long distance? It would take money to build a long telegraph line, and he had spent all his money. Morse went to Washington to ask Congress for some money. Day after day he sat in the visitors' gallery to see what Congress would do.

Finally the last day of the session arrived. The Congressmen would go home the next day. Morse waited till ten o'clock that night. The telegraph was not even mentioned. Morse went home. He was very much disappointed. Now, he would not be able to try his telegraph over a long distance.

In the morning Morse received good news. Congress had voted the money at midnight, in the last few minutes of the session. His telegraph line would be built after all.

The first telegraph line connected Washington and Baltimore. It was about 40 miles long. In 1844 Morse sent the first message over this line. It said, "What hath God wrought."

Telegraph lines soon connected all our biggest cities. By 1860 they reached the Mississippi River.

Attempts to Connect the Far West With the East. Until about 1850 when people talked about the West, they meant the region near the Mississippi River. Between 1850 and 1860 this region was connected with the Atlantic coast by roads, canals, railroads, and the telegraph. By this time there was a new West. Now the West was the Pacific coast: California and Oregon. Many settlers had gone to Oregon over the famous Oregon Trail. Many people had gone to California during the Gold Rush of 1849. Now the American people faced a new problem: How could California and Oregon be connected with the land east of the Mississippi River? This was a big problem because the Pacific coast is 2,000 miles from the Mississippi River.

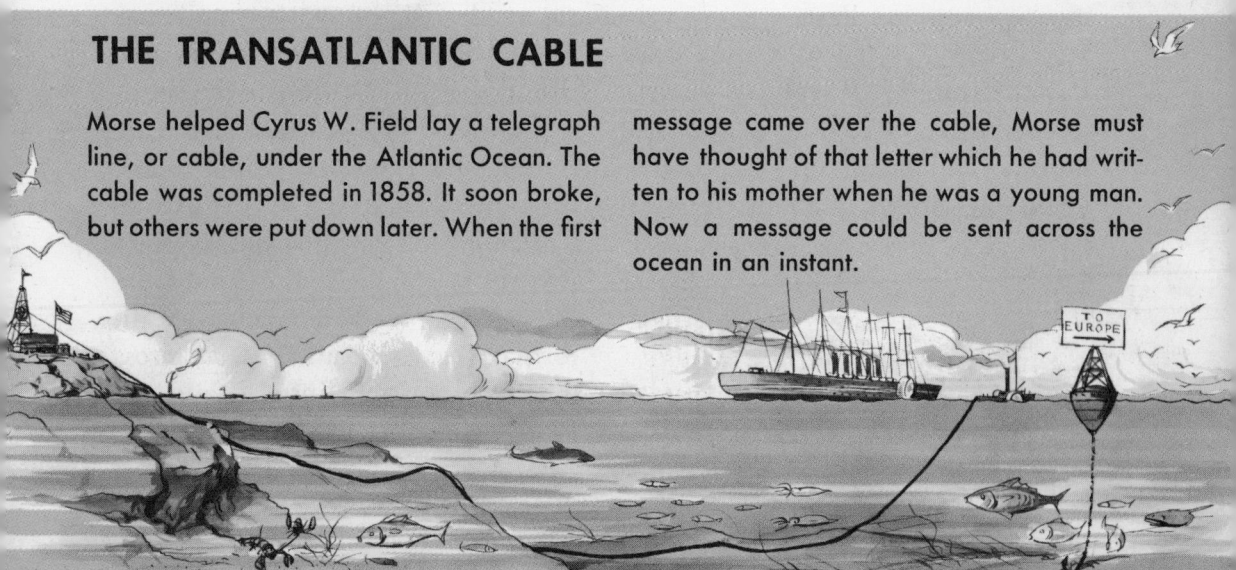

THE TRANSATLANTIC CABLE

Morse helped Cyrus W. Field lay a telegraph line, or cable, under the Atlantic Ocean. The cable was completed in 1858. It soon broke, but others were put down later. When the first message came over the cable, Morse must have thought of that letter which he had written to his mother when he was a young man. Now a message could be sent across the ocean in an instant.

In one way, building roads and railroads and telegraph lines west of the Mississippi was easier than it had been in the East. The route to the Pacific coast lay mostly across prairies and deserts. Trees did not have to be cut down as they did in the East. On the other hand, the Rocky Mountains had to be crossed, and they are much higher than the mountains in the East.

In 1858 a stagecoach line was started from St. Joseph, Missouri, to California. The line carried passengers and mail. A stagecoach made the journey in about 20 or 25 days.

The Pony Express. In 1860 a faster way was found to send mail to California. This was the famous Pony Express. A rider on a fast horse would carry the mail pouch for about 15 miles. Then he would quickly change to a fresh horse and ride for another 15 miles. At the end of 75 or 100 miles he would hand the mail pouch to another rider. In this way the mail was carried from St. Joseph, Missouri, to Sacramento, California, in about ten days. This was only half the time it took the stagecoach to make the same distance.

The Pony Express lasted less than two years. At the end of that time the telegraph had reached California. Messages could be sent across the country in an instant, and the Pony Express was no longer needed.

Railroads Span the Continent. Everyone knew that a railroad ought to connect the Pacific coast with the East. Two companies were formed to build the railroad. The Central Pacific was to begin in California and build toward the East. The Union Pacific was to begin at Omaha, Nebraska, and build toward the West.

The workers for the Central Pacific had great difficulties. The rails and other equipment had to be brought to California by boat, and the boats had to go all the way around South America. This railroad had to cross mountains and bridge deep gorges. Most of the work was done by Chinese laborers, called coolies.

The Union Pacific was built across the Great Plains. There was little water. Wood for the railroad ties had to be brought great distances. Even wood for campfires was scarce. The workers were always in danger from Indians. Most of the workers on this line came from Ireland.

In spite of all the difficulties, the work went on. On May 10, 1869, the two lines met near Ogden, Utah. A great crowd of people came to see the last spike driven into place. This spike was made of gold from California. There were speeches and a great celebration. The news was flashed by telegraph to every part of the United States. At last there was a railroad all the way across the United States. The East and the West were tied together by rails of steel.

Whitney's cotton gin, 1793.

THE COTTON GIN

Early gin in operation.

Whitney's assembly line.

Eli Whitney
Made History with His Inventions

Eli Whitney was born on a farm in Massachusetts. When he was a boy, he was handy with tools and made nails. The money he earned by making nails and by teaching paid his way through Yale College.

When he was 27, Whitney visited the South and saw cotton plants for the first time. He was told that if a way could be found to remove the seeds, the South could sell much cotton.

After eight months' work Whitney invented the cotton gin. He received little money for his invention. Others stole his idea. But the invention made cotton the biggest crop of the South.

Whitney was asked to manufacture guns for the government. Until this time all guns had been made by hand, and no two were exactly alike. Whitney's factory made parts exactly alike. Each part would fit any gun.

Today almost all manufacturers follow Whitney's plan of interchangeable, or standardized, parts. The parts are put together on an assembly line. This plan enables manufacturers to turn out products quickly and inexpensively and is called mass production.

Mass production has greatly changed the way Americans live and the way they work. Eli Whitney had no idea what he was starting when he built his gun factory back in 1798.

THE REAPER

Cyrus Hall McCormick
Brought Machines to the Farm

Cyrus McCormick lived on a farm in Virginia. At that time almost all farm work was done by hand. It took a long time to cut wheat, and much grain was lost. Cyrus and his father tried to build a machine that would cut wheat. The father gave up, but Cyrus continued to work on the idea.

In July, 1831, a crowd gathered to watch McCormick's new reaper. It worked! It cut the wheat quickly and evenly. Best of all, little grain was wasted.

McCormick felt that the prairies of the West would become the wheat-growing region of America. In order to be near the prairies, he decided to manufacture his reapers in Chicago, which was then a small city.

The McCormick reaper helped make America great and rich. We became the greatest wheat-growing country in the world. This could not have happened without a harvesting machine like the one Cyrus McCormick invented.

Before Cyrus McCormick died, his factories were turning out many kinds of farm machinery. Today's great machines do the work of many farmers, and do it better and faster.

Cutting wheat with scythes.

McCormick reaper of 1831

Modern combine harvester.

THE SEWING MACHINE

Howe's original machine.

Sewing machine of today.

An 1850 model.

Elias Howe
Invented a Sewing Machine

Elias Howe was born in Massachusetts. His father owned a farm and a mill. Neighboring farmers brought wheat to the mill to be ground into flour. Elias worked in the mill.

When he was 16, Elias went to work in Lowell, Massachusetts. Here he saw cotton being made into cloth in the textile mills.

There was plenty of cloth, but turning the cloth into clothing was long, hard work. Howe had an idea, he would build a machine to do the sewing.

Howe's tools were poor, and he had little money. He supported his wife and three children by odd jobs and worked on the sewing machine when he could find a little free time.

At last, in 1845, Howe had a sewing machine that worked. But his troubles were not over. At first people would not buy the machine. Then some manufacturers tried to steal his invention. Finally everything was straightened out. Howe received about $200,000 a year from sewing machine sales.

The first sewing machines were run by hand. Today most of them are run by electricity. Sewing machines are used in the home and in the factory. Some machines can sew canvas and other heavy materials. Some can even stitch leather. These are used to make boots and shoes.

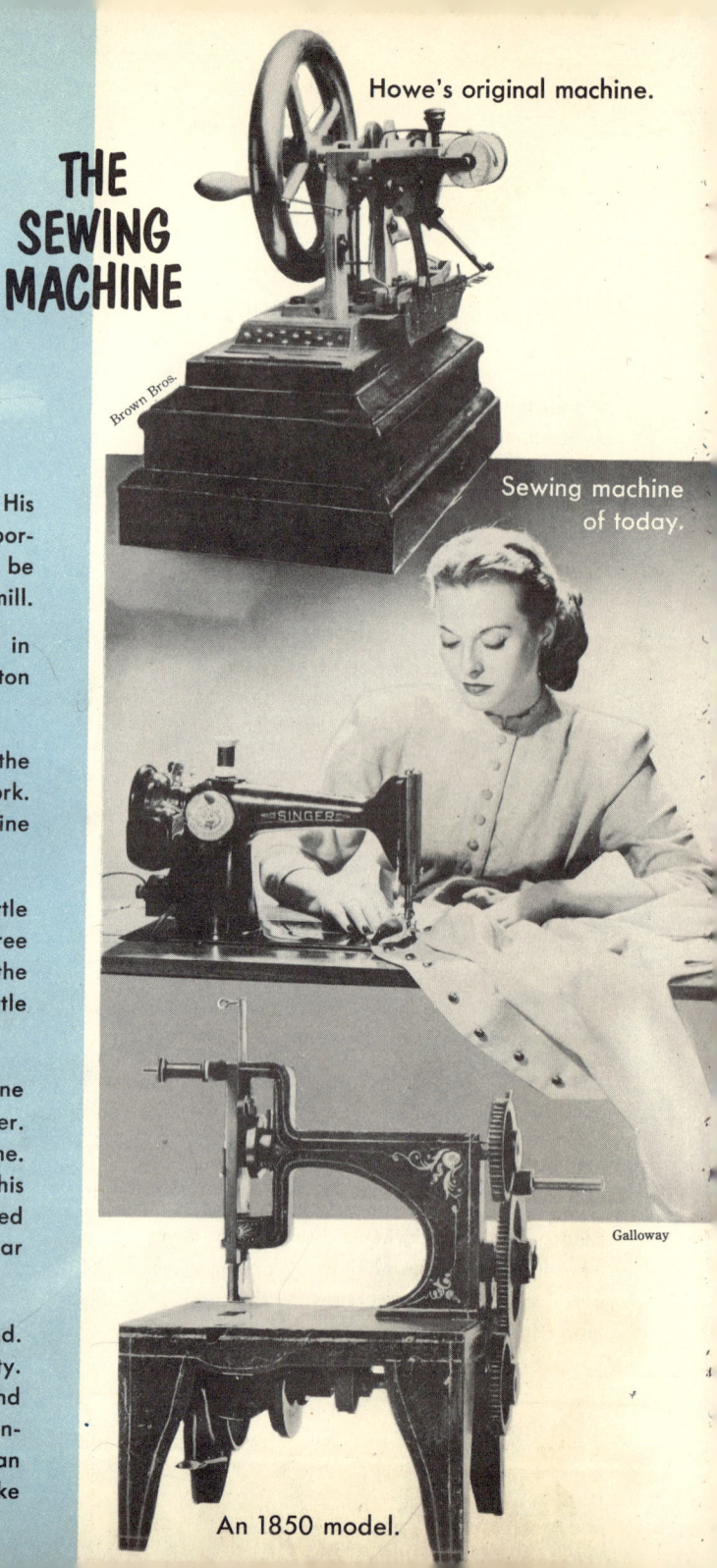

STUDY LESSON

WHERE IS IT? Answer each question in a complete sentence.

1. Where did most people live in the early days of America?
2. Where did most manufactured goods come from then?
3. Where was the Cumberland Road?
4. Where was Governor DeWitt Clinton's "Big Ditch"?

WHAT IS IT? Write each name and after it the phrase that explains it.

1. flatcars
2. transportation
3. *Great Western*
4. communication

a. sending messages
b. crossed the Atlantic using only steam in 1838
c. sending goods
d. railroad car with rude benches

WHO AM I? Write each man's name and after it the phrase that tells something about him.

1. Samuel Morse
2. Peter Cooper
3. Charles Carroll
4. Robert Livingston
5. DeWitt Clinton
6. Robert Fulton
7. James Watt

a. the Englishman who invented the steam engine
b. the U. S. Minister to France who helped Robert Fulton with the money he needed
c. the New Yorker who built the Erie Canal
d. the man who built the first steamboat
e. the Catholic who said that turning the first shovelful of earth for the Baltimore and Ohio Railroad was "the most important act of my life, next to signing the Declaration of Independence"
f. the man who built the first American steam locomotive, called the *Tom Thumb*
g. the successful artist who invented the telegraph

WORDS TO KNOW. Use each of these words in a sentence. Look them up in your dictionary unless you are sure of their meaning.

communication   transportation
coolies   telegraph
canal   toll

SOMETHING TO THINK ABOUT. Think carefully before you answer these questions.

1. How were people able to buy manufactured goods from Europe?
2. Why were people who lived inland so eager for better roads?
3. What was the greatest advantage of steamboat travel on the Hudson?
4. Why did DeWitt Clinton build the Erie Canal?
5. Why was the Baltimore and Ohio Railroad built?

265

GAMES...... ART.....

SCRAPBOOK OF FAMOUS PEOPLE

Each day you are learning about many famous people in history. Start now to write your own stories about them, and make a *Scrapbook of Famous People*. Put in it some of the great men and women you meet as you turn the pages of your history book. Find a picture to go with the story you write about your favorites. You can copy or trace the pictures you like. Here are two names to start your scrapbook.

Daniel Boone
John Charles Frémont

SOMEWHERE IN THE U. S. A

Draw or trace a map of the United States. Next, mark with heavy lines the Northwest Territory. Then put in with light lines the present boundaries of the states which were made from this territory, and letter the names of these states.

NAME GAME

Divide the class into two teams. Let one pupil give two clues about a person who has appeared in this section: "He started the first public library in Philadelphia; he wrote *Poor Richard's Almanac*." The first child on the other team must be able to solve the mystery name from the clues given. If he does not give the correct answer, "Benjamin Franklin," he is dropped from the team. When there are no members left on one team, the other team is the winner.

PRINCIPLES OF OUR FAITH

Write a letter to a pupil in a Communist nation and explain to him why the people of America honor George Washington and Patrick Henry. Show as clearly as you are able the difference between the things they were fighting for and the things many selfish leaders are fighting for in the world today. Explain how the ideas of freedom and justice have been the foundation of our American way of life from the very beginning.

BOOKS .... PLAYS

THIS IS HOW IT HAPPENED

PLAN A PLAY CALLED "PATHFINDER TO THE WEST"

Scene I:

Daniel Boone goes hunting in the woods in North Carolina. He meets his brother who is hunting with a friend. They are attacked by Indians but manage to escape.

Scene II:

Daniel Boone, his wife, and two brothers move to Kentucky and found the town of Boonesboro.

Scene III:

Boone and his companions are captured by the Indians, and Boone is adopted by the tribe. He later escapes and leads many settlers into the West.

WORKING TOGETHER

1. Several boys and girls can work together on this project. Use balsa wood or cardboard and make a model of the fort at Kaskaskia which George Rogers Clark captured from the British. You can find pictures of early forts in books in your library.

2. Do you know how many horses were used with the old stagecoaches? How many smokestacks did a Mississippi steamboat have? Let half the class draw or assemble a model stagecoach while the other half prepares a model or drawing of a river steamboat.

INFORMATION CENTER

If you had been one of the early settlers in the West, life would have been very different for you. What games would you have played? How would you have helped around the house and garden? What would you have studied? In the library you will find some excellent books on early American life. Here are a few to look for.

Phelan . . . . *Catholics in Colonial Days*
Johnston . . . . *Famous Scouts*
Earle . . . . *Child Life in Colonial Days*
Holberg . *At the Sign of the Golden Anchor*

Unit Seven
OUR NATION REMAINS UNITED

28. Slavery Divides the Nation

Slavery Lasted 250 Years. Here we see people working in a cotton field. These people are slaves. This means that they belong to the man who owns the cotton plantation. He owns the slaves just as he owns his horses and cows. He owns them just as he owns the plantation itself. The slaves must do exactly what he tells them. In return, he gives them their food, their clothes, and a place to live. He does not pay them any wages. If he wishes, he can sell the slaves. He can even sell members of one family to different buyers.

As we see in the picture, men, women, and children are all working. They are all slaves.

The man who is watching the slaves is an overseer. The overseer is paid by the plantation owner. His job is to see that the slaves keep working.

Today, there are no slaves in the United States. It is hard for us to believe that there was ever such a thing as slavery in our country. But slavery lasted for about 250 years. We shall see that slavery divided the country and led to a great war.

Why Slavery Was Important in the South. Slavery began in our country in 1619. In that year, a Dutch ship sailed into the harbor at Jamestown. The little settlement was only 12 years old at that time. The ship carried Negroes who had been stolen from their homes in Africa. These Negroes were sold to the plantation owners at Jamestown. The owners put the slaves to work in the tobacco fields. Cotton was not grown in our country at that time.

Jamestown is in Virginia, and Virginia is in the southern part of the United States. From the first, there were more slaves in the South than in the North. One reason for this was the warm climate of the South. The Negroes were accustomed to the warm climate of Africa. Another reason was that there were large plantations in the South, and many extra workers were needed.

From Jamestown, slavery spread to all parts of the South. In 1793, a young man named Eli Whitney invented the cotton gin. This was a machine which took the seeds out of cotton. After that, the plantation owners found they could make much money raising cotton. Slaves became more important than ever to the plantation owners because they needed many workers in the cotton fields.

How the Slaves Lived. We know that slavery leads to many evils. Human beings should not be bought and sold like animals. We also know that there were a few plantation owners who were cruel to their slaves.

Most plantation owners, however, were not cruel. They tried to see that the slaves were fairly happy.

Slaves usually lived in little huts or cabins. Many of them raised their own vegetables, chickens, and pigs. Their masters gave them presents now and then. Sometimes their

269

masters gave them a little spending money. Some of the slaves were allowed to have dogs and to go hunting in the master's woods.

In the evenings the slaves often sang and danced to the music of a banjo. The Negro slaves were the first people in America to use the banjo. It is believed that they brought it with them from Africa.

There were about 4,000,000 Negro slaves in the South in 1860.

Slave Owners Were Powerful. Most white people in the South did not own slaves. These people had small farms which they either owned or rented. They could not afford to keep slaves. They and their families did their own work on the farms.

There were also many people in the South who said that slavery was an evil thing. Some Southerners freed the slaves that they owned.

But most of the men who owned the big plantations believed that slavery was necessary. They were certain that they could not run their plantations without slaves. And these men were very powerful. They controlled the governments of the Southern states. They also had a big voice in the federal government. The plantation owners chose the men whom the Southern states sent to the House of Representatives and to the United States Senate in Washington. The Senate was evenly divided between the North and the South. No bill can become a law unless it passes both houses of Congress. The Southern senators usually could prevent a law from being passed if the plantation owners did not like it.

We see, then, that the Southern plantation owners were a small but powerful group. They were determined that no one was going to take their slaves away from them. As we shall see, they were also determined that slavery would spread into the territories owned by the United States.

Slavery Dies Out in the North. At one time there were a few slaves in the Northern states. But Northern farmers soon found that they could not use slaves. Most farms in the North were small. The family did all the work, and they did not need extra help. During the long winter months there was little work for the slaves to do. During these months the owners would have to provide a warm house and warm clothes for his slaves. The crops that were raised in the North needed very careful work. The Negro slaves were not trained to do this kind of work.

Many people in the North hated slavery. They said that no one should be allowed to own slaves. Since the farmers of the North did not wish to own slaves anyway, it was easy for these people to have their own way. In 1777 the legislature of Vermont passed a law doing away with slavery in that state. Soon, all the other Northern states had passed similar laws. The last one to do so was New Jersey in 1804.

After 1804 the United States was sharply divided on the question of slavery. The Northern states said that slavery was an evil thing and should not be allowed. The Southern states were controlled by men who said that slavery was absolutely necessary and must be continued.

Should Slavery Be Permitted in Territories? In the early 1800's most of the states of the Union were east of the Mississippi River. West of the Mississippi was the vast stretch of land which our country had bought from France. This land was divided into territories. The territories did not yet have enough people to be admitted into the Union as states. Congress made most of the laws for the territories. A question arose:

Should slavery be permitted in the territories?

Southern plantation owners answered "Yes" to this question. They wished to raise cotton in the Southern territories, and they said they could not do it without slaves.

Many Northern people said "No! Slavery is an evil thing. It will be hard to do away with slavery in the states where it already exists, but at least we can keep it from spreading. There must be no slavery in the territories."

This question of slavery in the territories caused much bitterness between the North and the South

Henry Clay

MISSOURI COMPROMISE

Should Missouri Be a Slave State or a Free State? In 1819 the people of Missouri asked to be admitted to the Union as a state. They had written a state constitution which permitted slavery in Missouri.

Most Northern Congressmen realized that if Missouri came into the Union as a slave state, a whole new region would be given over to slavery. The North believed that it must try to prevent the spread of slavery by refusing to let Missouri enter the Union except as a free state. Speeches were made and statements written to prove the evil of slavery.

Congressmen from the South were angry at this opposition. "The people of Missouri want slavery, and they should be free to choose slavery," these men said.

The Southerners had another reason for wishing Missouri to be a slave state. At that time there were eleven free states and eleven slave states. The Constitution says that each state should have two United States Senators, no matter how big or how small the state is. The Senate was evenly divided between the slave states and the free states. But if Missouri was admitted as a free state then there would be more Senators from the free states. The free states would always be in a position to outvote the slave states.

Henry Clay, a Senator from Kentucky, tried to work out a plan that would satisfy both the Northern and Southern Congressmen. In 1820, Maine asked to be admitted to the Union as a free state. Henry Clay suggested that Missouri be admitted as a slave state and that Maine be admitted as a free state. In this way there would still be an equal number of free and slave states. The Senate would still be evenly divided.

Henry Clay also had a plan for settling the question of slavery in the territories. He suggested that a line be drawn across the land that was bought in the Louisiana Purchase. Slavery would be permitted south of this line, but it would not be permitted north of this line.

Both houses of Congress followed Henry Clay's plan. Missouri came into the Union as a slave state, Maine came in as a free state, and the line was drawn across Louisiana.

When two opposing sides each give up part of what they want and come to an agreement, we say there has been a compromise. That is what the Southern Congressmen and the Northern Congressmen did in 1820. We call this the Compromise of 1820, or the Missouri Compromise.

For the next thirty years a free state and a slave state were always admitted at the same time. In 1850 there were 15 slave states and 15 free states.

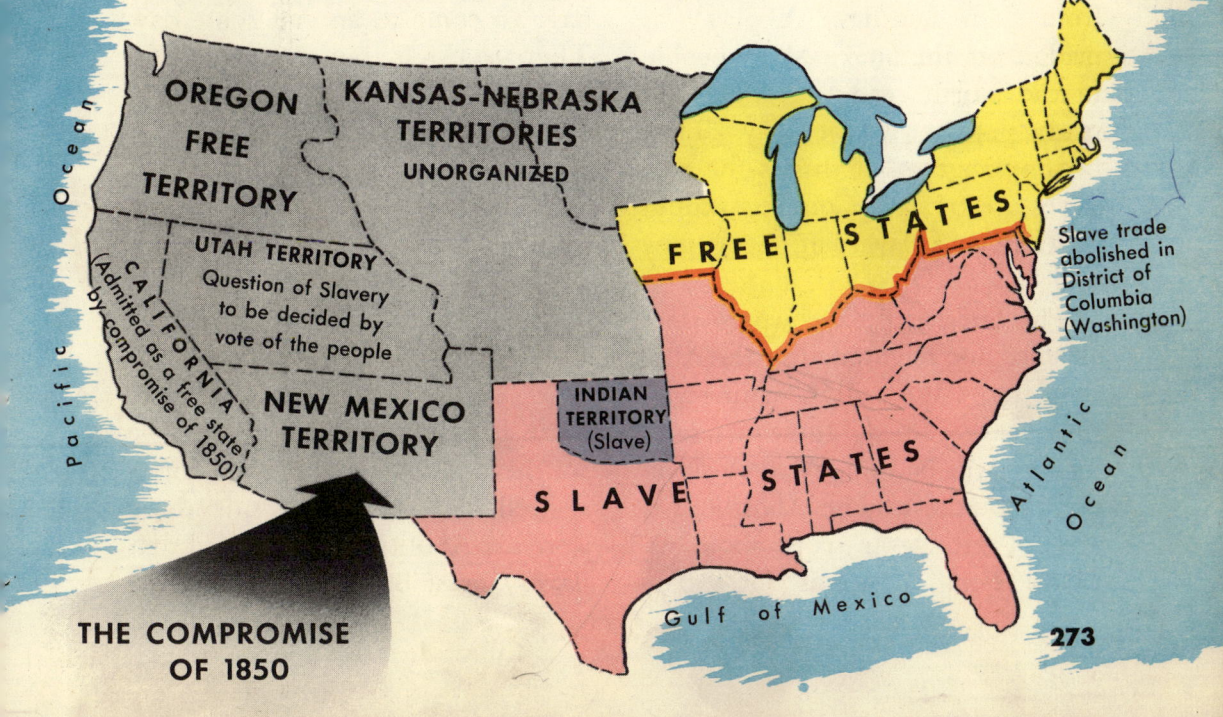

THE COMPROMISE OF 1850

Bitter Feeling Over Slavery. In the North there were some people who said that all slaves should be freed at once. These people were called Abolitionists. In the years between 1820 and 1860 the Abolitionists gained many followers in the North.

Harriet Beecher Stowe was an Abolitionist. She wrote a novel called *Uncle Tom's Cabin*. It was a story about slavery. In this story, slaves were beaten cruelly and separated from their families. A play was made from the book. Many people in the North read the book, and many people saw the play. They became angry. "If this is the way slaves are treated, Congress should do away with slavery at once," they said.

The Southern slaveowners were alarmed and frightened by the Abolitionists. "We will be ruined, if the slaves are freed," these men said. "There will be nobody to work on our plantations. The Abolitionists are not telling the truth about us. *Uncle Tom's Cabin* is not a true picture of the South. Most of us are very kind to our slaves."

Many people in the North felt that the Abolitionists went too far. "It is true that slavery is an evil thing," such people said. "But we must not end it too suddenly. This would not be fair to the slaves themselves or to the slaveowners. The slaves have not been educated. They would not know how to make a living if they were suddenly freed. They would have no homes and no food. And the plantation owners would be left no workers. They would lose many thousands of dollars. This is a very difficult problem and it cannot be solved quickly."

There were also many in the South who felt that slavery would have to come to an end some day. They, too, felt that this should be done slowly.

These reasonable people in the North and South might have been able to solve the problem had they been given the chance. As always, the trouble was caused by men on both sides who went to extremes: On the one side there were the plantation owners who said that slavery must be allowed not only in the Southern states but in the territories as well. On the other side there were the Abolitionists who said that slavery must be ended at once.

The Underground Railway. Sometimes slaves ran away from their masters. There was a law which said that slaves must be returned to their masters even if they escaped to a free state. But many people in the North did not pay any attention to this law. They helped the slaves escape. They hid the slaves in the daytime and helped them move on to another hiding place at night. This was called the Underground Railroad, although it was neither a railroad nor was it underground. Through the Underground Railroad, many slaves escaped to Canada. When they got there, they were free.

The Underground Railway was one more reason why there was bitter feeling between the North and the South. Plantation owners said that the Underground Railroad was causing them to lose slaves who were worth thousands of dollars. They said that Congress should pass a stronger law which would end the Underground Railroad.

May a State Leave the Union? The North and the South quarreled about other things besides slavery. We read in Chapter 22, that the North wished a high tariff and the South wished a low tariff. We read that in 1832 South Carolina thought the tariff passed by Congress was too high. Leaders of South Carolina said that they would take the state out of the Union if the federal government tried to collect the tariff. President Andrew Jackson said that South Carolina had no right to leave the Union. He called out the army. This trouble was settled peacefully. But there was still the question: May a state leave the Union?

Southerners said that a state could leave the Union. "After the former colonies won their freedom from Great Britain they were free and independent states," the Southerners said. "We came into the Union of our won free will. We may leave it of our own free will any time we wish."

"Furthermore," some of the Southerners said, "if the North continues to make trouble over slavery and tariffs, we may leave the Union very soon."

"No," said most Northerners. "You may not do that. Once a state comes into the Union, it is in for good. It has no right to leave."

The Compromise of 1850. At the end of the Mexican War, in 1848, the United States secured a vast new territory from Mexico. This territory caused more trouble between the North and the South.

"Slavery must be permitted in this territory," said the Southerners.

"Slavery must not be permitted in this territory," said the Northerners.

While Congressmen were still talking about this, California asked to be admitted to the Union. The people of California wished their state to be a free state. The constitution that they had written declared that there would be no slavery in the state of California.

The Southerners did not wish to admit California as a free state. This would give the free states more votes than the slave states in the Senate.

Henry Clay was still in the Senate at that time. He was called the Great Peacemaker, because he had often brought about peace between the North and the South.

Once again Clay suggested a plan that he hoped would satisfy both sides. Some points in his plan favored the North. Other points favored the South. He made a great speech begging Congress to accept the plan. Congress did so. This was called the Compromise of 1850.

The chief points of the Compromise of 1850 (see page 273) were:

1. California came into the Union as a free state.

2. The rest of the land taken from Mexico was divided into two territories. The people in these territories were to decide for themselves whether to come into the Union as slave or free states.

3. A new law was passed which made it harder for the Northerners to help escaped slaves.

The peace brought by the Compromise of 1850 lasted only a short time. Henry Clay died in 1852. He did not live to see the war between the North and the South.

"Bleeding Kansas." In 1854 Congress passed a law which caused much trouble. This was the Kansas-Nebraska Act. The law said that the people living in the territories of Kansas and Nebraska could decide for themselves whether or not they wanted slavery.

Northerners were angry when the bill was passed. Kansas and Nebraska were north of the Missouri Compromise line of 1820. Everyone had thought that this compromise closed to slavery forever the territories north of this line. Even the Southerners had thought so. Now, Congress said that the people must vote on the question.

Everyone was sure that Nebraska would be a free state because it was so far to the north. Both sides tried to secure Kansas. Northerners who were against slavery started an organization to send to Kansas settlers who opposed slavery and who would vote to keep it out. Southerners in Kansas saw that they were going to be outnumbered. They tried to keep Northerners from entering the territory. Fighting broke out. People on both sides were killed.

People called the territory "Bleeding Kansas."

For the first time, Americans were actually fighting each other over the question of slavery, and lives were being lost. In the years to come, many more lives would be lost.

The Dred Scott Decision. Dred Scott was a Negro slave. His master took him from the slave state of Missouri to the free territory of Minnesota. After they lived there for a while, Dred Scott's master took him back to Missouri.

Dred Scott then claimed that he was no longer a slave. He said that he was now free because he had lived in Minnesota which was free territory according to the Missouri Compromise.

The case was carried to the Supreme Court of the United States. In 1857 the Supreme Court ruled that Dred Scott was not free. The court said that Congress had no right to prohibit slavery in Minnesota or any other territory.

Southern plantation owners were delighted. This meant that slavery was permitted in all the territories owned by the United States.

Northerners were disappointed and angry. The decision of the United States Supreme Court was a great defeat for the enemies of slavery.

Republicans Oppose the Spread of Slavery. Before 1854 the two big political parties in the United States were the Democrats and the Whigs. These parties each had followers in both the North and the South. Neither party said very much about slavery, because they did not wish to lose votes in either section.

In 1854 a new political party was organized. It was the Republican party. The Republican Party announced that it was opposed to the spread of slavery. The Republicans said they would not try to do away with slavery in the states of the Old South. But they insisted that there must be no slavery in the territories and that all new states entering the Union must be free.

Very few Southerners joined the Republican Party, but many Northerners joined. They were glad to have a party that took a strong stand on slavery.

In 1860 the Republicans nominated Abraham Lincoln of Illinois as their candidate for President of the United States.

The Southern leaders warned: "If Abraham Lincoln is elected President, the Southern states will leave the Union."

When the votes were counted, it was found that Lincoln had been elected. Would the Southern states carry out their threat? Would they leave the Union? In the next chapter we shall read what happened.

STUDY LESSON

WHERE IS IT? Answer each question in a complete sentence.

1. Where in our country did slavery begin?
2. What state was the first to do away with slavery?
3. What state did Henry Clay represent in Congress?
4. Where did the Underground Railway take the slaves?
5. Where did Abraham Lincoln live before he became President?

WHAT IS IT? Write each name and after it the phrase that explains it.

1. Missouri Compromise
2. Abolitionists
3. *Uncle Tom's Cabin*
4. Underground Railroad
5. Dred Scott Decision

a. an escape route to the North for runaway slaves
b. Supreme Court ruling saying that Congress could not prevent slavery in any territory
c. Henry Clay's plan adopted in 1820
d. a novel written to show the evils of slavery
e. Northerners who wished to do away with slavery at once

WHO AM I? Write each name and after it the phrase that tells something about the person.

1. Eli Whitney
2. Henry Clay
3. Harriet Beecher Stowe
4. Dred Scott

a. author of *Uncle Tom's Cabin*
b. famous Negro slave
c. Senator from Kentucky who offered the Missouri Compromise plan
d. inventor of the cotton gin

WORDS TO KNOW. Use each of these words in a sentence. Look them up in your dictionary unless you are sure of their meaning.

Abolitionist   tariff
compromise   decision

SOMETHING TO THINK ABOUT. Think carefully before you answer these questions.

1. Why was slavery popular in the South and unpopular in the North?
2. Why was the Missouri Compromise important?
3. Why was there trouble in Kansas around 1854?
4. Why was the Dred Scott Decision a blow to people who were opposed to slavery?
5. How did the Southern states feel about the election of Abraham Lincoln?

29. The Civil War

Abraham Lincoln. In the last chapter we read that Abraham Lincoln was elected President of the United States in 1860.

Abraham Lincoln was born in a log cabin on a poor Kentucky farm on February 12, 1809. When he was seven years old his father took the family across the Ohio River to the backwoods of Indiana. "It was a wild region," Lincoln said later, "with many bears and other wild animals in the woods." Two years later, when Lincoln was nine, his mother died. He missed her very much.

There were few schools in the backwoods. Young Abe was able to spend only about one year in school. He had to walk four miles through the forest to reach the school. He was very eager to learn, so he taught himself. At night he lay on the floor of the cabin and read by the light of the fire. Paper was scarce, so he wrote and worked problems on the back of a shovel. He used a burnt stick for a pencil.

As a young man, Abraham Lincoln worked very hard. His father needed help to support the family. For a while, Abe earned money by splitting rails for fences. That is why he was later called "the rail splitter." Before he was 21, Lincoln was six feet four inches tall. Hard work had given him a strong body with powerful muscles.

In 1830 the Lincolns set out by ox team and covered wagon for a new home in Illinois. Here, Abe Lincoln had many different jobs. At times he worked as a mill hand. For a while he was a clerk in the village store. He served as postmaster and worked as a surveyor. While he was doing all these things he studied law books in his spare time. When he had learned enough about the law, he became a lawyer.

People liked Abraham Lincoln because he was kind and honest. They also knew that he was a very wise person. The people elected him to help make laws in the Illinois state legislature. They also sent him to Washington as a member of the House of Representatives.

Lincoln Becomes President. Stephen A. Douglas was the United States Senator from Illinois. Douglas had a small body and a powerful mind. He was called the "Little Giant." Douglas had many followers. They hoped that some day Douglas would be President of the United States.

Douglas was a Democrat. In the election of 1858 the Republicans of Illinois chose Abraham Lincoln to run against Douglas for the Senate. Lincoln invited Douglas to speak from the same platform with him. Douglas was one of the most powerful speakers of his time, and he was glad to accept the invitation. The two men debated about the problems of the day. These debates are called the Lincoln-Douglas debates.

In 1858 the whole country was interested in the problem of slavery. The people of Illinois wanted to know what these two candidates thought about slavery. Lincoln had one great advantage here. He knew

281

exactly where he stood on the slavery question. He said that slavery should not be allowed in the territories. Almost all the Republicans felt this way. That was the chief reason why the Republican Party had been organized.

Douglas, on the other hand, had to try to please all the Democrats. That meant the Democrats of the North who disliked slavery and the Democrats of the South who favored slavery.

Lincoln lost the election for Senator, but he had attracted the attention of the whole country. People of the North liked his clear, strong arguments against slavery. In 1860 the Republicans nominated Abraham Lincoln for President. The Democrats were hopelessly divided. The Northern Democrats nominated Lincoln's old opponent, Stephen A. Douglas. The Southern Democrats nominated another man. There was great excitement during the campaign. Southern leaders said they would not accept Lincoln as President even if he were elected. As we read in the last chapter, they said the Southern states would leave the Union if Lincoln were elected.

When the votes were counted, it was found that Lincoln had been elected.

The Southern States Leave the Union. A month after Lincoln was elected, South Carolina declared that it was no longer part of the United States. Within a few weeks six more Southern states voted to leave the Union. Delegates from the seven states met at Montgomery, Alabama. They formed a government which they called the Confederate States of America.

Jefferson Davis was elected President of the Confederate States of America. Jefferson Davis and Abraham Lincoln had been born in the same county in Kentucky. Abraham Lincoln had moved to Indiana and Illinois which were free states. Jefferson Davis moved to Mississippi, which was a slave state. Davis lived on a large plantation with many slaves. The slaves were well-treated. Davis could not believe that slavery was wrong.

Davis went to college and later entered the United States Military Academy at West Point. He made a good soldier. He fought bravely during the Mexican War. After the war he was elected to the Senate of the United States. He also served as Secretary of War.

Fighting Begins. President Lincoln said that no state had a right to leave the Union. He said that the Confederate States were not really a new country.

Jefferson Davis

Nevertheless, the Confederate States acted as though they were an independent nation. They took over all United States property within the borders of the Confederacy. One piece of United States property was Fort Sumter. This fort was on an island near Charleston, South Carolina. Its commander was Major Robert Anderson of the United States Army. A Confederate general ordered Anderson to surrender the fort. He refused. Then at 4:30 in the morning of April 12, 1861, the Confederates fired on Fort Sumter. Major Anderson was forced to surrender the fort.

UNION AND CONFEDERATE STATES

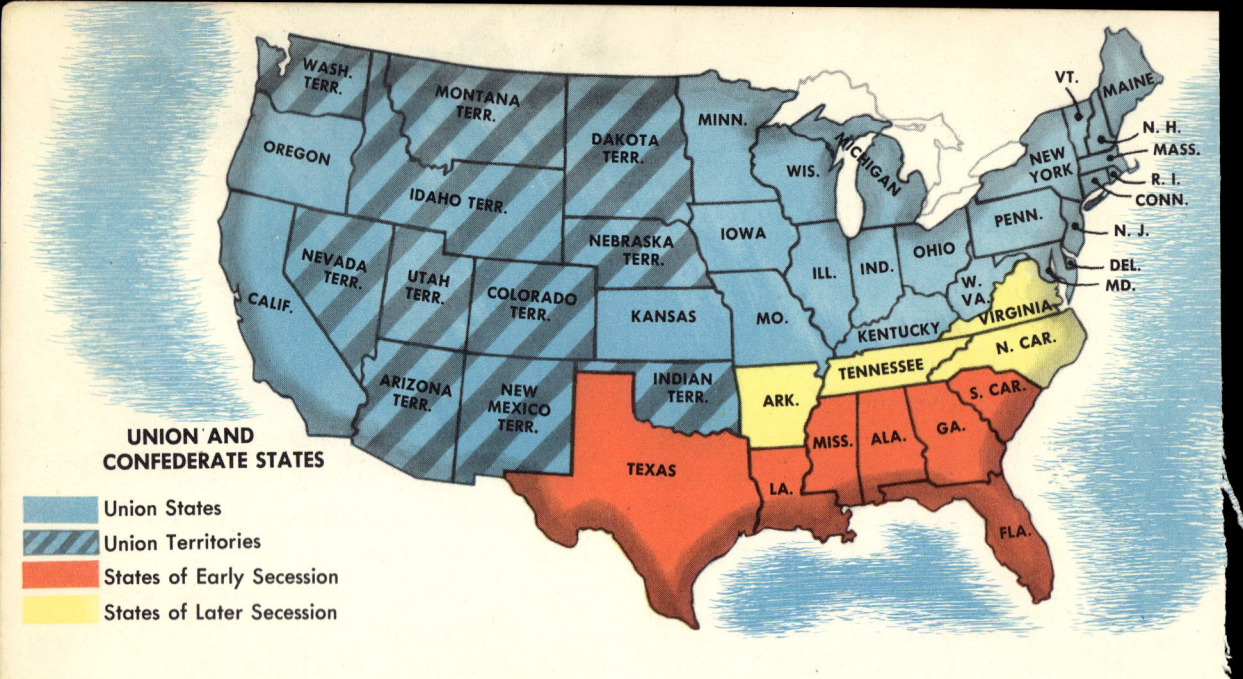

- Union States
- Union Territories
- States of Early Secession
- States of Later Secession

This was the first battle in the war between the North and the South. Usually this war is called the Civil War. Sometimes it is called the War between the States.

After the fall of Fort Sumter, four more Southern states joined the Confederacy. This made eleven states in the Confederate States of America. Twenty-three states remained loyal to the United States of America.

Virginia Gives the Confederate States a Capital and a Great General. Virginia was one of the states that joined the Confederacy after the fall of Fort Sumter. The capital of the Confederacy was then moved from Montgomery, Alabama, to Richmond, Virginia. Richmond remained the capital of the Confederacy until the end of the Civil War.

Virginia also gave the Confederacy its greatest general, Robert E. Lee. Robert E. Lee came from one of Virginia's finest families. He graduated from West Point and had a fine record as a soldier.

Lee did not believe in slavery. He said it was a great evil. He loved the United States Army. He had a fine chance of being put at the head of the United States Army during the Civil War.

But Virginia had joined the Confederacy, and Lee thought it was his duty to fight for his state. "How can I draw my sword upon Virginia, my native state?" he asked himself. So he resigned from the United States Army and joined the army of the Confederacy.

A Nation Divided. The Civil War brought sad days to our country. Thousands of fine young men were killed. More thousands were wounded. Farms and orchards were destroyed. Homes and barns were burned to the ground. People were left homeless and penniless.

Northern soldiers fought bravely to save the Union. They were called the "boys in blue" because of the color of their uniforms.

Confederate soldiers fought just as hard for their native states and for the Confederacy. They were called the "boys in gray" because of the color of their uniforms.

At first sight it seemed that the North could win easily. There were about 22 million people in the North. There were only 9 million people in the South, and 4 million of these were slaves. The North had much greater wealth. It had factories which could make guns and cannons and supplies for the army. It could build all the ships it needed.

The South had few factories, and no shipyards. The South was a land of farms and plantations.

But the North found that it was not easy to win the war. A Union army set out to capture the Confederate capital of Richmond. The army was badly beaten in the Battle of Bull Run.

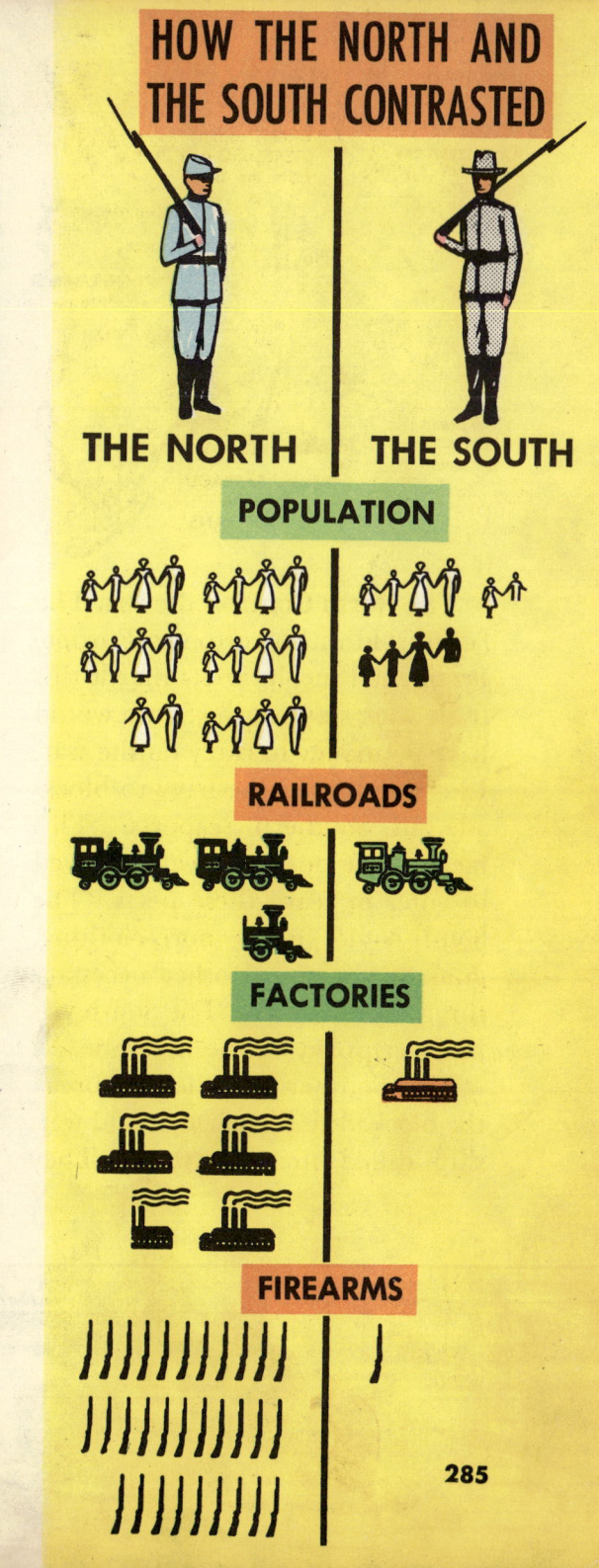

HOW THE NORTH AND THE SOUTH CONTRASTED

THE NORTH | **THE SOUTH**

POPULATION

RAILROADS

FACTORIES

FIREARMS

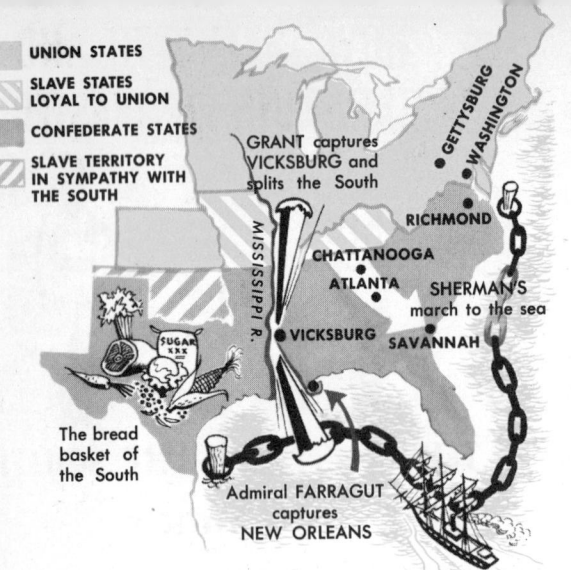

Map legend:
- UNION STATES
- SLAVE STATES LOYAL TO UNION
- CONFEDERATE STATES
- SLAVE TERRITORY IN SYMPATHY WITH THE SOUTH

Map labels: GRANT captures VICKSBURG and splits the South • GETTYSBURG • WASHINGTON • RICHMOND • CHATTANOOGA • ATLANTA • SHERMAN'S march to the sea • MISSISSIPPI R. • VICKSBURG • SAVANNAH • The bread basket of the South • Admiral FARRAGUT captures NEW ORLEANS

The North Controls the Sea. The South sold much cotton to Europe. President Lincoln knew that if this trade were stopped the South would have no money to carry on the war. Lincoln ordered the navy to blockade all Southern seaports. This meant that no ships were allowed to enter or leave these ports. The South could get no more clothing, guns, medicine, or other necessary things from abroad. The South was badly crippled by the blockade.

The Southerners tried to break the blockade. They had an old warship called the *Merrimac*. They covered the ship with iron plates. Then the *Merrimac* sailed forth to meet the wooden warships of the United States Navy. The Northern ships were not able to harm the *Merrimac*. Cannon balls bounced harmlessly off the iron sides of the ship. For a time it looked as though the *Merrimac* would be able to break the blockade.

But the North also had an iron-clad vessel. It was called the *Monitor*. The *Monitor* floated very low in the water. It had a round gun turret. The Confederates called it "a cheese box on a raft."

The two ironclads met in battle. Neither could sink the other. The battle was a draw. But the South could not build many ironclads. The North could build all that were needed. The North was able to keep up the blockade.

The battle between the *Monitor* and the *Merrimac* showed the value of iron-clad ships. It meant that the days of the wooden sailing vessels would soon come to an end. Today all ships are made of steel.

The Confederacy Is Cut in Two. The commander of the Union army in the Upper Mississippi Valley was General Ulysses S. Grant. Like Lee, Grant had been graduated from West Point.

Early in 1862 Grant attacked Fort Donelson in western Tennessee. The Confederate commander saw he was beaten and tried to make easy terms of surrender. Grant said: "No terms except unconditional and immediate surrender can be accepted." The fort was surrendered. This earned Grant a new nickname, "Unconditional Surrender" Grant.

The Southern states that were west of the Mississippi were called the Breadbasket of the South. They supplied much of the food for the Confederacy. President Lincoln planned to cut the South in two by capturing all the land along the Mississippi River.

The South had built a great fort at Vicksburg on the Mississippi. General Grant was sent to capture the fort. This was a difficult job, but it was well carried out. On July 4, 1863, Vicksburg surrendered. Within a short time the North had control of the entire Mississippi River. The Breadbasket of the South was cut off from the rest of the Confederacy.

General Lee Is Defeated at Gettysburg. Most of the battles had been fought on Southern soil. General Lee decided to invade the North. In the early summer of 1863 he led his army into Pennsylvania. He hoped that he might lead the army to Baltimore or Philadelphia, or even on to New York.

General George Meade was in command of the Union army that was ordered to stop Lee. The two armies faced each other near the town of Gettysburg, in Pennsylvania, on July 1, 1863. The armies fought furiously for two days. On the third day General Lee decided to risk all on one great attack. It

HOW THE WAR WAS FOUGHT---

And Those Who Fought It

Soldiers used horse-drawn cannons, muskets, swords—no atom bombs, tanks, or fast jet planes.

The North won at Gettysburg but Lincoln was sad to see the graves.

Gen. Sherman hastened the end of the war by ruining Confederate territory and gave Savannah to Lincoln as a Christmas gift.

Gen. Jackson's army stood like a stone wall at Bull Run and the South won twice.

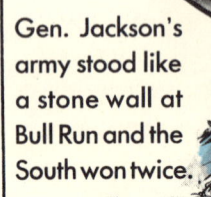

With cannons still barking at the front, these soldiers were helping their wounded and dying buddies to reach a hospital tent.

Atlanta was cleared of civilians, then burned, at the beginning of Sherman's famous march to the sea.

Gen. Grant said: "I am more a farmer than a soldier," but he led the Union to victory.

Gen. Lee said: "Do your duty in all things. You cannot do more.. Never wish to do less."

Holy Cross Sisters under Mother Angela, set up hospitals to nurse the wounded.

was one of the boldest attacks in history. With their officers in front, the "boys in gray" swept across the battlefield at Gettysburg. They moved through a sweeping rain of shot and shell.

The attack failed. The Confederate army was defeated. Lee led his shattered army back into Virginia.

This was the day before General Grant sent word that he had captured Vicksburg. This gave the North control of the Mississippi and split the Confederacy. The South had received two terrible blows.

The Slaves Are Freed. On New Year's Day, 1863, President Lincoln announced that all slaves were free in the states fighting the United States. This was called the Emancipation Proclamation. Lincoln freed these slaves because he thought this might help win the war.

The Emancipation Proclamation freed thousands of slaves, but it did not end slavery in the United States. There were still slaves in Kentucky, Missouri, Delaware, and Maryland. These were slave states but they were not fighting the United States. There were also slaves in some of the territories. There was nothing to prevent the former Confederate states from having slavery after they came back into the Union.

The End of the War. Lee's army held off Union victory for two more years. Before that time, President Lincoln put General Grant in command of all the Union armies. Grant had twice as many men as Lee. He planned to keep fighting and to give the Confederate soldiers no rest. "I propose to fight it out ... if it takes all summer," Grant said. It took not only all summer but all winter, too.

The South was nearly exhausted. General William T. Sherman had captured Atlanta on September 2, 1864. He marched from that city to the sea. As he marched, he destroyed everything that stood in his path.

Richmond fell at last to the Union soldiers on April 2, 1865. Lee tried to lead his small, half-starved army toward the mountains. He was cut off by Union armies. There was nothing for him to do but surrender. Lee met Grant at Appomattox Court House, in Virginia. It was April 9, 1865.

The two men talked for a short time about their days in the Mexican War. Then Grant wrote out the surrender papers. Lee signed them.

Lee asked that the soldiers be allowed to keep their horses and mules. Grant said that they could do so, because they would need them "to help in the spring plowing."

The two men parted. Lee mounted his horse and rode off to say goodbye to his soldiers.

Within a few weeks all the other Confederate armies had surrendered. The war was over.

Results of the Civil War. The Civil War had three very important results.

1. The Union was saved.
2. It was settled that no state had the right to leave the Union.
3. The question of slavery was settled. The 13th Amendment to the Constitution abolished slavery in the United States.

In January 1865 Congress passed the 13th Amendment to the Constitution. This amendment said that slavery shall not exist in the United States. Before an amendment can go into effect, it must be approved by three-fourths of the states. The Southern states could have blocked this amendment if they had all been in the Union. But 11 states were out of the Union, so the amendment was approved. It became part of the Constitution on December 18, 1865.

Since that day it has been against the law to own slaves in any part of the United States of America.

STUDY LESSON

WHERE IS IT? Answer each question in a complete sentence.

1. What state elected Lincoln to the House of Representatives?
2. Where was Fort Sumter?
3. Where was the first capital of the Confederacy? Where was the capital finally established?
4. Where was the home of Robert E. Lee?
5. Where did the South suffer its greatest defeat?
6. What state did Sherman destroy as he marched to the sea?
7. Where was the final surrender signed?

WHAT IS IT? Write each name and after it the phrase that explains it.

1. Confederacy
2. Emancipation Proclamation
3. *Merrimac*

a. the Confederate ironclad ship which tried to break the blockade
b. the President's order freeing the the slaves
c. the group of Southern states which left the Union

WHO AM I? Write each name and after it the phrase that tells about him.

1. Stephen Douglas
2. William Tecumseh Sherman
3. Jefferson Davis
4. Major Robert Anderson
5. General George Meade

a. President of the Confederacy
b. commander of Fort Sumter
c. defeated Lee at Gettysburg
d. defeated Lincoln in election to Senate
e. captured Atlanta and marched to the sea

WORDS TO KNOW. Use each of these words in a sentence. Look them up in your dictionary unless you are sure of their meaning.

blockade   independent
nominate   amendment
abolish

SOMETHING TO THINK ABOUT. Think carefully before you answer these questions.

1. What helped Lincoln in the election campaign for President?
2. Why did the Southern states oppose a Republican President?
3. How many states were members of the Confederacy? How many remained loyal to the Union?
4. Why do you think the North won the war? Give at least three advantages the North had in the war.
5. How did the North try to shorten the war?
6. How did Lincoln plan to cut the South in two?
7. What were three important results of the Civil War?

INDEX

A

Abolitionists (ăb′ȯ·lĭsh′ŭn·ĭsts), 274
Adams (ăd′ămz), John
  as President, 191
  First Continental Congress, 162
Adams, John Quincy (kwĭn′zĭ), 207, 212
Adams, Samuel
  Committee of Correspondence formed by, 160
  First Continental Congress, 162
  taxes and, 159
Africa, 32-33, 35, 136
  Diaz reaches the tip of, 36
  Da Gama rounds, 46
  New England trade with, 136
Airplanes, 331, 369, 375
  first trans-Atlantic flight, 331
Alabama (ăl′ȧ·băm′ȧ)
  admitted into the Union, 220
  settled by cotton farmers, 219
Alamo (ăl′ȧ·mō), the, 225, 226
Alaska (ȧ-lăs′kȧ), 318
  purchased from Russia, 309, 310-311
  riches of, 310
Albany (ôl′bȧ·nĭ), New York, 92, 95, 170, 252, 253
Albemarle (ăl′bĕ·märl), 126
Algonquin Indians (ăl·gŏng′kĭn), 78, 79
Allen, Ethan (ē′thăn ăl′ĕn), 163
Allies (ă·līz′), 345, 346
Amendments, constitutional (kŏn′stĭ·tū′shŭn·ăl ȧ·mĕnd′mĕnts)
  Bill of Rights, 182-183
  13th, 290
  14th, 295
America, naming of, 49
American Indians, 5-6, 43, 44, 45, 69, 70, 71, 90, 91, 92
  discover America, 12
  gifts of, 13
  in French and Indian War, 148-149
  in Kentucky, 217
  in Mexico, 58-61
  in Oregon, 242
  in Plymouth, 106
  in South America, 63
  in the Southwest, 11
  in Virginia, 69, 70, 71
  in the West, 298, 299-300
  life of, at California missions, 232-233
  naming of, 43
  Penn and, 120
  Plains, 10-11
  Spain's treatment of, 64-65
  See also Algonquin Indians; Aztec Indians; Creek Indians; Huron Indians; Inca Indians; Iroquois Indians; Seminole Indians; Shawnee Indians; Sioux Indians
American Revolution, see War for Independence
American Samoa (sȧ·mō′ȧ), 317, 318
Amsterdam (ăm′stēr·dăm), Fort, 115
Anchorage (ăng′kēr·ĭj), Alaska, 309
Anderson (ăn′dēr·s'n), Major Robert, 283
André (än′drā), Major John, 174
Angela, Mother M., 289
"Apostle of the Alleghanies, the," see Gallitzin, Demetrius
"Apostle of the Rockies, the," see De Smet, Peter, S.J.
Appalachian Mountains (ăp′ȧ·lăch′ĭ·ȧn), 194, 216, 217
Appomattox Court House (ăp′ȯ·măt′ŭks), 290
Arizona (ăr′ĭ·zō′nȧ), 228, 300
  admitted into the Union, 307
Ark, the, 124
Arkansas (är′kăn·sô), 240
  admitted into the Union, 222
Arkansas Territory, 220
Arnold, Benedict (bĕn′ĕ·dĭkt är′n'ld)
  country betrayed by, 174-175
Assemblies (ȧ·sĕm′blĭz), colonial, 74, 118, 137, 158
  the first, in America, 74
Assembly line, 262, 330
Astrolabe (ăs′trȯ·lāb), the, 34
Atchison (ăch′ĭ·s'n), Kansas, 305
Atlanta (ăt·lăn′tȧ), Georgia
  captured during Civil War, 288, 290
Atlantic Cable (ăt·lăn′tĭk), the, 259
Atom bombs (ăt′ŭm bŏmz), 358, 375
Atomic power (ȧ·tŏm′ĭk), 327
Auriesville (ôr′ēs·vĭl), N. Y., 80
Austin, Moses (mō′zĭz ôs′tĭn), 223
Austin, Stephen, 223, 224
Austin, Texas, 223
Austria (ôs′trĭ·ȧ)
  World War I, 345
Automobiles, 329-330, 333
  first American automobile powered by gasoline, 329
  Ford's first automobile, 330
Aviation (ā′vĭ·ā′shŭn), 331
Axis nations (ăk′sĭs), 354, 355
Aztec Indians (ăz′tĕk), 58-59

B

Bacteria (băk·tēr′ĭ·ȧ), 332
Badin (bä′dăn′), Father Stephen, 362
Bahamas (bȧ·hä′măz), 43
Balboa (băl·bō′ȧ), discovers Pacific Ocean, 50
Baltimore (bôl′tĭ·mōr), Maryland
  British attempt to capture, 204
  St. Mary's College and Seminary in, 362
Baltimore, Lord, 125, 126
Baltimore and Ohio Railroad, 257
Barge (bärj) defined, 255
Barry (băr′ĭ), Captain John, 171-172
Bases (bās′ĕz), military, 318, 356
  in Alaska, 311
  in Hawaii, 312
  on Guam, 314, 356
Battles, see names of battles
Bay of Fundy (fŭn′dĭ), 350
Bayley (bā′lĭ), Elizabeth Ann, see Seton, Elizabeth Ann
Bear Flag, 235
Bear Flag Republic, 235
Bell Alexander Graham (grā′ăm), 328
Belleau Wood (bĕl′ō′), 347
Bering Strait (bēr′ĭng strāt), 311
Berkeley (bûrk′lĭ), Lord, 118
Bessemer (bĕs′ĕ·mēr), Henry, 324-325
Bessemer converter (kŏn·vûr′tēr), 324
Bill of Rights, 182-183
Black Robes, 80, 82-85
Blackfish, Chief, 218
Blast furnace, 324
"Bleeding Kansas," 277
Blessed Virgin appears, 60-61
Boats, Northmen's, 14-15
Bon Homme Richard (bôN′ŏm′ rē′shär′), 172

iii

Bookmaking, 20, 34
Boone, Daniel (dăn'yĕl boōn), 173, 216-219, 220, 222
Boone, Jemima (jê·mī'ma), 217
Boonesborough (boōnz'bû·rô), Kentucky, 173, 217, 218
Boston (bôs'tŭn), Massachusetts, 159, 160, 161, 162, 163, 164, 165, 170
  port of, closed by British, 161
  settlement of, 107
  Washington drives British from, 164
"Boston Massacre" (măs'a·kẽr), 159
Boston Tea Party, 160-161
Braddock (brăd'ŭk), General Edward, 149-150
Bradford (brăd'fẽrd), Governor William, 103, 104, 105
Branding, cattle, 305
Braves, Indian, 8, 125
Brazil (bra·zīl'), 206
Breadbasket of the South, 287
Breed's Hill, 164
British Columbia (kô·lŭm'bĭ·a), 245
Buena Vista (bwā'nä vēs'tä), battle of, 227
Buffaloes (bŭf'a·lōz), 197, 298, 299
Bulgaria (bŭl·gâr'ĭ·a)
  World War I, 345
Bull Moose Party, 342
Bull Run, battle of, 285, 288
Bunker Hill (bŭng'kẽr), battle of, 164
Burgoyne (bûr·goin'), General John, 170
Burr (bûr), Aaron, 202

C

Cabot (kăb'ŭt), John, 48-49, 68, 146
Cabrillo, Juan (hwän kä·brē'(l)yō), 230
Cabrini, Mother Francesca (fränchăs'kä ka·brē'nê), 364, 366
California (kăl'ĭ·fôrn'ya), 65, 228, 230-239, 259, 260, 261, 298
  admitted into the Union, 236, 273
  becomes American territory, 234-235
  discovered, 230
  Gold Rush, 235-236, 259
  missions, 231-233, 234
  Spaniards in, 230-231
Calvert (kăl'vẽrt), Leonard, 125

Camino Real, El (ĕl kä·mē'nō rä·äl'), 232
Canada (kăn'a·da), 170
  U. S. attempt to capture, 203, 204
Canal Era (ē'ra), 255
Canal Zone (zōn), 316-317
Cans, tin, 325
Cape of Good Hope, 36
Cape Verde (vûrd), 35
"Capital" (kăp'ĭ·tăl), defined, 191
"Capitol" (kăp'ĭ·tŏl), defined, 191
Captains of industry, 332-334, 340
Carnegie (kär·nā'gĭ), Andrew, 333
Carolinas (kăr'ô·lī'naz), the, 126
"Carpetbaggers" (kär'pĕt·băg'ẽrz), 295, 296
Carroll (kăr'ŭl), Charles, 257, 360, 361
Carroll, Daniel, 179
Carroll, John, 360-362
Carteret (kär'tẽr·ĕt), George, 118
  Governor Philip, 118
Cartier (kàr'tyā'), Jacques, 77
Carver (kär'vẽr), Governor John, 105
Catholic Church
  and the American Indians, 9, 59-61, 64-65, 80-85
  Cortez and, 59
  friend of the workingman, 334
  in England, 102
  in Greenland, 17
  in Maryland, 124-126
  in New Jersey, 118
  in Pennsylvania, 120, 131
  in the United States, 360-368
  Our Lady of Guadalupe, 60, 61, 65
  Prince Henry and the, 35
  Spanish settlers and the, 64-65, 66. *See also* Catholic religion; Catholic schools; Catholics
Catholic religion
  as France's gift, 80-85
  and the Northmen, 16, 17
  as Spain's gift, 64-65, 66
Catholic schools
  in the United States, 366-367
Catholics
  at Constitutional Convention, 179
  in Maryland, 124, 126
  in Pennsylvania, 120
  in War for Independence, 171, 173, 175

  See also under names of, e.g., Saint Frances Xavier Cabrini, Peter De Smet, Demetrius Gallitzin, etc.
Cattle, 304-305
Cattlemen, 305, 306
Central America, 206
Central Pacific Railroad, 261
Central Powers, 345
Champlain (shăm·plān'), founds Quebec, 78-89
Chapultepec (chä·poōl'tâ·pĕk'), Mexico, 228
Charleston (chärlz'tŭn), South Carolina, 126, 283
  captured by British, 175
Château-Thierry (shä'tō'tyē'rē'), 347
Chemistry (kĕm'ĭs·trĭ), 332
Chesapeake Bay (chĕs'a·pēk), 69
Chicago (shĭ·kô'gō), Illinois, 325
Chillicothe (chĭl'ĭ·kŏth'ê), Ohio
  Indian camp at, 218
Christina (krĭs·tē'na), Fort, 94, 95
Church of England, 102, 103, 140
Civil War, the, 280-290
  results of, 290
  states of early secession, 284
  states of later secession, 284
Civilian Conservation Corps (sĭ·vĭl'yăn kŏn'sẽr·vā'shŭn kôr), 353
Clark (klärk); George Rogers, 173-174, 196, 219
Clark, William, 173, 196-198
Clay (klā), Henry, 273, 276
Clemenceau, Georges (zhôrzh klä'män'sō'), 348
Clermont (klẽr'mŏnt) (steamboat), 252-253
Cleveland, Grover (grō'vẽr klĕv'lănd), 312, 345
Clinton, De Witt (dĕ wĭt' klĭn't'n), 254-255
Coal, 322
Coal miners, 322
Colombia (kô·lŭm'bĭ·a), 316
Colonial assemblies, 158
Colonists (kŏl'ô·nĭsts)
  declare freedom, 167-176
  effect of French and Indian War on, 153
  explained, 146
Colony (kol'ô·nĭ)
  explained, 70
Colorado (kŏl'ô·rä'dō), 198, 228, 303
Columbia River (kô·lŭm'bĭ·a), 197, 242

iv

Columbia University, 188
Columbus (kŏ·lŭm′bŭs), 6, 26, 37, 38-45
  discovers America, 38-45
  importance of, 44, 46
Committees of Correspondence (kŏ·mĭt′ĭz ŏv kŏr′ê·spŏn′dĕns), 160, 161, 163
Communication (kŏ·mū′nĭ·kā′shŭn)
  defined, 247
  telegraph, 258-259
  telephone, 328
  television, 328
Communism (kŏm′ů·nĭz′m), 373-376
Communists (kŏm′ů·nĭsts), 372-376
Compromise of 1820 (kŏm′prŏ·mīz), 273, 277, 278
Compromise of 1850, 273, 276
Concord (kŏng′kĕrd), Massachusetts, 170
  seized by British, 162, 163
Conestoga wagons (kŏn′ĕs·tō′gȧ), 249
Confederate States of America (kŏn·fĕd′ĕr·ĭt), 282-290, 292, 294, 295
Congress (kŏng′grĕs)
  First Continental, 161-162
  origin of, 179-180, 185
  Second Continental, 164, 165, 167, 174, 194
Congress of Industrial Organizations, 334
Connecticut (kŏ·nĕt′ĭ·kŭt), 110
Connecticut River, 170
Constitution (kŏn′stĭ·tū′shŭn), United States
  acceptance of, 182-183, 185
  Amendments, 182
    Bill of Rights, 182-183
    13th, 290
    14th, 295
  first written, 110
  origin of, 179, 181
Constitutional Convention (kŏn′stĭ·tū′shŭn·ȧl kŏn·vĕn′shŭn), 178-183
Continental Congress (kŏn′tĭ·nĕn′tăl)
  First, 161-162
  Second, 164, 165, 167, 174, 194
Coolidge, Calvin (kăl′vĭn kōō′lĭj), 351
Cooper (kōō′pĕr), Peter, 257
Corduroy roads (kôr′dŭ·roi), 248
Cornwallis (kôrn·wŏl′ĭs), General Charles, 169, 170, 175, 176

Coronado (kō′rŏ·nä′tho), Francisco
  searches for "Seven Cities," 64
Corporations, 332-333, 340
Cortez (kôr′tĕz), Hernando
  conquers Aztecs, 58-59
Cotton, 138, 140, 219-220, 224, 269, 286, 296
Cotton gin (jĭn), 219, 262, 269
Cowboys, 304-305
Crazy Horse, Chief, 300
Creek Indians, 210
Crusades (krōō·sādz′), 20-26
Cuba (kū′bȧ), 318
  independence granted to, 314
  Spanish-American War, 313-314, 339
Cumberland (kŭm′bēr·lănd), Maryland, 249
Cumberland Gap (găp), 217
Cumberland Road, 249
Custer (kŭs′tēr), George, 300

D

Da Gama (dȧ gă′mȧ), Vasco
  reaches Far East first, 46
Dare (dâr), Virginia, 126
Davis (dā′vĭs), Jefferson, 283
Dawes (dôz), William, 162
DC-7, 331
Declaration of Independence, 165, 167, 187, 194, 257, 360
De Forest (dĕ fŏr′ĕst), Lee, 328
DeKalb, Baron Johann (yŏ·hän′ dĕ kälb), 175
Delaware (dĕl′ȧ·wâr)
  and Penn, 121
  Swedes and Dutch settle, 94
Delaware River, 170, 172
  Washington retreats across, 169
"Democracy" (dĕ·mŏk′rȧ·sĭ), defined, 194
Democratic Party, 278, 281, 282
Democratic-Republicans, 189
Depressions (dĕ·prĕsh′ŭnz), 351-352
Desert Trail, 249
De Smet (dĕ smĕt′), Peter, S. J., 244
De Soto (dĕ·sō′tō), Hernando
  discovers the Mississippi, 63, 83
Dewey (dū′ĭ), George, 313, 314
De Witt Clinton (locomotive), 256
Diamond Head Mountain, Hawaii, 312
Diaz (dē′ȧs), Bartolomeu
  rounds Africa's tip, 36

Diego, Juan (hwän dē·ā′go), 60-61
Diesel-electric locomotive (dē′zĕl), 256
Dirigible (dĭr′ĭ·jĭ·b′l), 346
Discovery of America
  by Europeans, 42-43
  by Indians, 12
District of Columbia
  founded, 190
  slave trade abolished in, 273
Donelson (dŏn′l·s′n), Fort, 287
Dongan (dŏn′găn), Governor Thomas, 117
Dorchester Heights (dôr′chĕs′tēr), 164
"Doughboys," (dō′boiz′), 346
Douglas (dŭg′lăs) Lewis W. (lū′ĭs), 374
Douglas, Stephen A., 281-282
Dove, the, 124
Drake, Edwin (ĕd′wĭn drāk), 323
Drake, Sir Francis, 231
"Drake's Folly," 323
Dred Scott decision (drĕd skŏt), 278
Duquesne (dōō·kan′), Fort, 149-150
Dutch in New York, 90-92, 95, 114-116
Dutch, Pennsylvania, 120
Dynamo (dī′nȧ·mō), Edison's, 327

E

Edison, Thomas Alva (ăl′vȧ ĕd′ĭ·s′n), 326-327
Edward (British warship), 171
Eisenhower, Dwight D. (dwīt ī′z′n·hou′ēr), 356, 375
El Camino Real, see Camino Real, El
Electric light bulb
  invented by Edison, 327
Electricity, 322, 326, 328
Elizabeth (ê·lĭz′ȧ·bĕth), N. J.
  beginning of, 118
Emancipation Proclamation (ê·măn′sĭ·pā′shŭn prŏk′lȧ·mā′shŭn), 289
Embargo Act (ĕm·bär′gō), 202
Emerson, Ralph Waldo (rălf wôl′do ĕm′ēr·s′n), 163
Emmitsburg (ĕm′ĭts·bûrg), Maryland
  first American headquarters of the Sisters of Charity, 364
England (ĭng′glănd), see Great Britain

v

Ericson, Leif (lāv ĕr′ĭk·s'n), 15-18, 44
 finds North America, 17
Eric the Red, 15
Erie (ēr′ĭ), Lake, 254, 255
Erie Canal, 249, 254-255
European Recovery Plan, 374
Executive branch (ĕg·zĕk′ū·tĭv),
 of federal government, 181
Explorers
 Dutch, *see* Hudson
 English, *see* Cabot
 French, *see* Cartier, Champlain, La Salle, Marquette, *and* Verrazano
 Italian, *see* Cabot, Columbus, Marco Polo, Vespucci, *and* Verrazano
 Portuguese, *see* Diaz, Da Gama, *and* Prince Henry's sailors
 Spanish, *see* Columbus, Coronado, Magellan, Pizarro, *and* Ponce de Leon

F

Factories, 202, 285, 321, 322, 324, 328, 332, 333, 355
Fairbanks, Alaska, 309, 310
Far East, 23, 28-30, 32, 35, 46, 51, 52, 90, 91
 Da Gama reaches, 46
 in trade, 23, 26
 Magellan reaches, 51
 Marco Polo in, 28-31
 Prince Henry's interest in, 35
Farmer, Father (Ferdinand Steinmeyer), 118
Farmers
 colonial, 130-131, 132-133, 134, 140
 cotton, 219-220
 New Deal and, 354
 prairie, 306
 See also Southern planters
Fatima, *see* Our Lady of Fatima
Feast of the Immaculate Conception (ĭ·măk′ū·lĭt kŏn·sĕp′shŭn), 356
Federal government, 180-181
 branches of, 181
 powers of, 181
Federalists (fĕd′ẽr·ăl·ĭsts), 189
"Fifty-four forty or fight," 244
Film studio, first, 326
First Continental Congress, 161-162
Fishermen
 French, in New World, 76
 New England, 136

Fitz-Simons (fĭt(s)·sī′mŭnz), Thomas, 179
Florida (flŏr′ĭ·dà), 64
 bought from Spain, 211
 Jackson invades, 210-211
Foch, Marshal Ferdinand (fûr′dĭ·nănd fôsh), 347
Ford, Henry, 329-330
Ford Motor Company, 330
Ford's Theater, 293
Forts, *see* names of forts
France (frans)
 aided Americans in War for Independence, 171, 175
 French and Indian War, 156
 Louisiana Territory purchased from, 195
 World War I, 345, 347
Franciscan missions, 65
Franciscans (frăn·sĭs′kănz), 230, 232, 233
Franklin, Benjamin (bĕn′ja·mĭn frăngk′lĭn)
 Constitutional Convention, 180
 First Continental Congress, 162
 tried to persuade Canadians to join American side in the Revolution, 361
Freedom of religion
 in Maryland, 124-126
 in New Jersey, 118
 in Pennsylvania, 119, 131
 in Providence, 109
 none in England, 102-103
 none in New England, 108
 none in the South, 140
Frémont (frē′mŏnt), John, 234
French and Indian War, 146-153, 156, 185
 effects of the, 153
Fulton (fool′t'n), Robert, 252, 321
"Fulton's Folly," 252
Fundamental Orders of Connecticut, 110
Fundy (fŭn′dĭ), Bay of, 350
Fur trade
 French, 78, 79, 84
 in New York, 92-93, 115, 126, 130

G

Gadsden (gădz′dĕn), Fort, 211
Gadsden Purchase (1853), 229
Gage (gāj), General Thomas, 161, 162, 164
Gaillard Cut (gĭl·yärd′), 316, 317
Gallitzin, Demetrius (dē·mē′trĭ·ŭs ga·lĭt′sĭn), 362

Gasoline, 323
Gatun Locks (ga·tōōn′), 317
Genoa (jĕ′nō·a), Italy, 25, 30, 48
 merchants of, 25, 38
George III, King, 158, 159, 165
Georgetown College (jôrj′toun), 362
Georgia (jôr′ja), 127-128
German settlers, 120-121
Germantown, Pa., 120-121
Germany (jûr′ma·nĭ)
 in World War I, 345, 347
 in World War II, 354, 356, 357
 U. S. declares war on, 345
Geronimo (jĕ·rŏn′ĭ·mō), 300
Gettysburg (gĕt′ĭz·bûrg), Pennsylvania
 battle of, 287-289
Gibault, Father Pierre (pyär zhē′bō′), 173
Gold
 discovered in California, 235-236
 discovered in Colorado, 303
 in Alaska, 310
Gold Rush (1849), 235-236, 259
Goliad (go′lĭ·ăd′), Texas, 225, 226
Gompers (gŏm′pẽrz), Samuel, 333
Goodyear (good′yẽr), Charles, 332
Gorgas (gôr′găs), Colonel William, 317
Government, *see* Assemblies; Constitution; Federal government; State government
Grand Trunk Railway, 326
Grant, Ulysses S. (ū·lĭs′ēz)
 as President, 294
 Civil War days, 286, 287, 289, 290
 in Mexican War, 228
Great American Desert, 298
Great Britain
 American Revolution, 162-165, 167-176
 California claimed by, 231
 colonies taxed by, 156-161
 French and Indian War, 156
 Oregon claimed by, 243, 244
 Parliament, 156, 157, 158, 159, 161
 War of 1812, 203-205
 World War I, 345, 347
Great Khan (kän), 28-30
Great Lakes, 79, 82, 88, 253
Great Plains, 261
Great Western (steamship), 253
"Green Mountain Boys," 163

vi

Greenland (grēn′lănd)
Northmen in, 15, 16, 17
Guadalupe, see Our Lady of Guadalupe
Guam (gwŏm), 314, 318, 356
Guerrilla warfare (gĕ·rĭl′à), 175
Gutenberg (gōō′tĕn·bĕrк), John, 34
Guthrie (gŭth′rĭ), Oklahoma, 307

H

Hale, Nathan (nā′thăn hāl), 168
Half Moon, the, 90
Hamilton, Alexander (ăl′ĕg·zăn′dẽr hăm′ĭl·tŭn)
death of, 202
Secretary of the Treasury, 186, 187-188, 189
Harding, Warren (wŏr′ĕn här′dĭng), 351
Harrodsburg (hăr′ŭdz·bûrg), Kentucky, 217
Hartford (hart′fẽrd), Conn.
founding of, 110
Havana (há·văn′à), Cuba, 313
Hawaii (há·wī′ê), 311-312, 318
Hayes, Rutherford B. (rŭth′ẽr fẽrd hāz), 296
Helicopter (hĕl′ĭ·kŏp′tẽr), 331
Henderson (hĕn′dẽr·s'n), Richard, 216
Henry, Patrick, 162, 193
Henry of Portugal, Prince, 32-35, 36
Hessians (hĕsh′ănz), the, 169
Hiroshima (hē′rŏ·shē′má), Japan
atom bomb dropped on, 358
Hitler, Adolf (ăd′ŏlf hĭt′lẽr), 354, 355, 373
Holland (hŏl′ănd), 171
Holy Cross Sisters, see Sisters of the Holy Cross
Holy Wars, 20-26
Homes, colonial, 115-116, 134, 139
See also Houses
Homestead Act (hōm′stĕd), 306
Honolulu (hŏn′′l·ōō′lōō), Hawaii, 312
Hooker (hŏŏk′ẽr), Thomas
founds Connecticut, 110
Hoover, Herbert (hûr′bẽrt hōō′vẽr), 352
Horses, 329, 330
Hospitality (hŏs′pĭ·tăl′ĭ·tĭ), Southern
explained, 139

House of Burgesses (bûr′jĕs·ĭz), 193, 194
House of Representatives
origin of, 180
Houses, Dutch, 115-116
colonial, 130-131
New England, 134-135
Southern, 139
Swedish, 94
Houston (hūs′tŭn), Sam, 226
Howe, Elias (ê·lī′ăs hou), 264
Howe, General Richard, 170
Hudson (hŭd′s'n), Henry
discovers Hudson River, 90-91
Hudson River, 170, 174, 252, 253, 255
Hudson's Bay Company, 241-243
Huron Indians (hū′rŏn), 78, 80

I

Iceland (īs′lănd)
discovery by Northmen, 15
Idaho (ī′dá·hō), 303
admitted into the Union, 245
Illinois (ĭl′ĭ·noi′), 174, 219, 283
admitted into the Union, 220
Immigration (ĭm′ĭ·grā′shŭn), 365
Inca Indians (ĭng′ká)
Pizarro conquers, 63
Independence, Missouri
Oregon Trail began at, 240
Indian reservations, 299-300, 306
Indian wars, 300
Indiana (ĭn′dĭ·ăn′á), 174, 219, 280, 283
admitted into the Union, 220
Indians, 5-6, 43, 44, 45, 69, 70, 71, 90, 91, 92
Algonquin, 78, 79
Aztec, 58-59
Blessed Virgin and, 60-61
Creek, 210
discover America, 12
gifts of, 12-13
Huron, 78, 80
in French and Indian War, 148-149
in Kentucky, 217
in Mexico, 58-61
in Oregon, 242
in Plymouth, 106
in South America, 63
in the Southwest, 11
in Virginia, 69, 70, 71
in the West, 298, 299-300
Inca, 63
Iroquois, 78, 80, 149

life of, at California missions, 232-233
naming of, 43
Penn and, 120
Plains, 10-11
Seminole, 211
Shawnee, 217-218
Sioux, 300
Spain's treatment of, 64-65
See also under given names, e.g., Chief Crazy Horse, Juan Diego, etc.
Indo-China (ĭn′dŏ·chīná)
Communists gain control in, 374
Industry, captains of, 332-334, 340
Iowa (ī′ô·wà)
admitted into the Union, 222
Iron, 324
Iroquois Indians (ĭr′ô·kwoi), 78, 80, 149
Irrigation, 340-341
Italy (ĭt′l·ĭ)
World War I, 345, 347
World War II, 356
Iwo Jima (ē′wō jē′má), 357

J

Jackson (jăk′s'n), Andrew
as President, 212-215, 275
battle of New Orleans, 205
campaigns against the Seminoles, 211
early life of, 209-211
Jackson, Fort, 211
Jackson, Hugh (hū), 210
Jackson, Robert, 210
Jackson, T. J. ("Stonewall"), 228, 288
James, I, King of England, 69
Jamestown (jāmz′toun), Virginia
founding of, 68-72, 124
slavery began at, 269
Japan (já·păn′)
in World War I, 345
in World War II, 354, 355-356, 358
Jefferson (jĕf′ẽr·s'n), Thomas
as President, 193-198, 201-203, 344
Declaration of Independence written by, 165, 187, 194
early life of, 193-194
Secretary of State, 186, 187, 188, 189, 194
Vice-President, 194
Jerusalem (jê·rōō′sá·lĕm), Israel, taken by Crusaders, 24

Jesuit martyrs (jĕz′û·ĭt), 80
Jogues (zhôg), Saint Isaac, 80
John, King of Portugal, 36
Johnson (jŏn′s'n), Andrew, 294
Joliet (zhô′lyĕ′), Louis, 83-84
Jones (jōnz), John Paul, 172
Joseph, St., 334
Judicial branch (jōō·dĭsh′ăl), of federal government, 181
Juneau (jōō′nō), Alaska, 309, 310

K

Kansas-Nebraska Act (kăn′zăs nĕ·brăs′kȧ), 277
Kansas-Nebraska Territories, 273
Kaskaskia (kăs·kăs′kĭ·ȧ), Fort, 173
Kateri Tekakwitha (kȧ·tĕr·ê tĕk′ȧ·kwĭth′ȧ), 81
Kearney (kär′nĭ), Colonel Stephen, 235
Kelly, William, 324
Kentucky (kĕn·tŭk′ĭ), 173
 admitted into the Union, 220
 exploration and settlement of, 216-217
Kerosene (kĕr′ô·sēn′), 323
Ketchikan (kĕch′ĭ·kăn′), Alaska, 310
Key (kē), Francis Scott, 204
Khan (kän), Great, 28-30
King's College, 188
Kitchens, colonial
 Dutch, 116
 New England, 135
 Pennsylvania, 130-131
Kitty Hawk (kĭt′ĭ·hôk′), North Carolina, 331
Kitty Hawk (airplane), 331
Knights of Labor (nīts), 333, 334
Knox (nŏks), Henry, 186, 187
Korea (kô·rē′ȧ)
 war in, 375
Kosciusko, Thaddeus (thăd′ê·ŭs kŏs′ĭ·ŭs′kō), 175

L

Labor, 333-334
Labor unions, 333-334
Lafayette, Marquis de (mȧr′kē′ dē lä′fĭ·ĕt′), 175
Lake Erie
 battle of, 204
La Salle (lȧ·săl′), René de, 86-87, 146
Lawrence, James, 205
League of Nations, 347, 348, 350-351, 370, 371

Lee, "Light Horse Harry," 174
Lee, Robert E., 228, 284, 287, 289, 290, 293
Legislative branch (lĕj′ĭs·lā′tĭv), of federal government, 181
Lend-Lease Act (lĕnd′lēs′), 355
L'Enfant, Pierre Charles (pyȧr shȧrl län′fän′), 190
Leo XIII, Pope, 334
Lewis (lū′ĭs), John L., 334
Lewis, Merriwether (mĕr′ĭ·wĕth′ ẽr), 196-198
Lewis and Clark Expedition, 196-198
Lexington (lĕk′sĭng·tŭn) (ship), 171
Lexington, Kentucky, 217
Lexington, Massachusetts, 170
 battle of, 162-163, 216
Liberty Bonds, 347
Life
 Crusades change, 26
 in 11th century Europe, 20
 in English colonies, 130-140
 in a French colony, 154
 in Middle colonies, 115-116, 130-133
 in the Near East, 23
 in New England, 134-136
 in New Netherland, 115-116
 in Southern colonies, 138-140
 in a Spanish colony, 66
Liliuokalani (lê·lê′wô·kä·lä′nê), Queen, 311-312
Lincoln, Abraham (ā′brȧ·hăm lĭng′k'n)
 early life of, 280-281, 338
 elected President, 278, 280, 282, 338
 murdered, 293
 nominated for President, 278, 282
 ordered navy to blockade Southern seaports, 286
 plan for the South after the Civil War, 293, 294
 second term as President, 293
 slaves freed by, 289
Lincoln-Douglas debates, 281
Lindbergh (lĭn(d)′bûrg), Charles A., 331
Livingston (lĭv′ĭng·stŭn), Robert, 252
Locomotives (lō′kô·mō′tĭvz), steam, 256, 257, 321, 329
Los Angeles (lŏs ăn′jĕl·ĕs), 64
Louisiana (lōō′ĭ·zĭ·an′ȧ), 240
 admitted into the Union, 222
Louisiana Purchase, 195-196, 222
Louisiana Territory, 196, 229

M

MacArthur (măk·är′thẽr), General Douglas, 356, 358
Machine Age, 320-334
Madison (măd′ĭ·s'n), James, 203
Magellan (mȧ·jĕl′ăn), Fernando, 50-52
Main Highway, the, *see* Camino Real, El
Maine (mān) (battleship), 313
Manhattan Island (măn·hăt′ăn), 90, 92, 115
Manila (mȧ·nĭl′ȧ), Philippine Islands
 captured in Spanish-American War, 313
Manila Bay, battle of, 314
Manufacturing (măn′û·făk′tûr· ĭng)
 U. S. leads the world in, 321
Maps
 Africa, Diaz rounds, 36
 Alaska, 309
 Boone's trail, 217
 Cabot's voyage, 48
 Camino Real, El, 232
 Cartier's voyage, 77
 Champlain's voyages, 79
 Civil War, the, 286
 Clark's route, 173
 Columbus, first voyage of, 45
 Compromise of 1850, the, 273
 Crusades, the, 21
 Diaz rounds Africa, 36
 Dutch in New York, the, 91
 English plan to defeat the Americans, the, 170
 English possessions, 96
 "Fifty-four forty or fight," 243
 forty-eight states, the, 308
 French possessions, 88, 96
 Hawaiian Islands, the, 312
 Indians of North America, the, 10, 12
 Jackson's campaigns against the Seminoles, 211
 Louisiana Territory, the, 196
 Magellan circles the world, 52
 Main Highway, the, 232
 Marquette's explorations, 85
 Maryland, 125
 Mexico and Texas, the area disputed by, 227
 Middle Colonies, the, 122
 Missouri Compromise, the, 272
 New England, 108, 112
 North America after 1763, 152
 Northmen's voyages, the, 14
 Ohio country, the, 147

viii

Panama Canal, the, 317
Portugal in the New World, 62
possessions and territories, United States, 318
railroads span the continent, 261
roads and trails, early American, 249
Southern colonies, the, 128
Spain in the New World, 62, 96
territories and possessions, United States, 318
Texas, the settlement of, 224
Texas and Mexico, the area disputed by, 227
trade routes, Old World, 29
trails and roads, early American, 249
Triple Alliance and the Triple Entente, the, 346
Union and Confederate states, 284
United States in 1819, the, 220
United States in 1853, the, 229
Verrazano's voyage, 77
Virginia and Maryland, 125
voyages, 14, 45, 48, 77, 85
Washington, D.C., 190
World War II, the theaters of war in, 357
Marco Polo, *see* Polo, Marco
Marconi, Guglielmo (gōō·lyĕl′mȯ mär·kō′nė), 328
Marines (mȧ·rēnz′), 357
Marquette (mär·ket′), Father Jacques, 82-85
explores Mississippi, 83-84
"Marriage of the Waters," 255
Martyrs
French, 80, 81
Indian girl, 81
Spanish, 64-65
Maryland (mĕr′ĭ·lănd), Catholic colony of, 124-126
Massachusetts (măs′ȧ·chōō′sĕts), 209
colony, 161, 162
Massachusetts Assembly, 161
Massachusetts Bay Colony, 104, 107-108
Massachusetts Bay Company, 107
Massacre, Boston, *see* Boston Massacre
Massasoit (măs′ȧ·soit′), Chief, 106, 109
Mass production, 262
Matanuska Valley (măt′ȧ·nōōs′kȧ), Alsaka, 311
Mayflower (mā′flou′ẽr), the, 104
Mayflower Compact, the, 105

McCormick, Cyrus Hall (sī′rŭs mȧ·kôr′mĭk), 263
McKinley (mȧ·kĭn′lĭ), William, 312, 313, 339
McLoughlin (măk·lok′lĭn), Dr. John, 241-243, 244
Meade (mēd), General George, 287
Meat Inspection Act, 340
Merchants, 25, 28, 38
Merchant ships
in the Revolutionary War, 178
Merrimac (mĕr′ĭ·măk) (warship), 286
Mexican Cession (sĕsh′un) (1848), 229
Mexican War, 227-228, 235, 276, 283, 287, 326
Mexico (mĕk′sĭ·kō), 206, 222-229
history of, 58-62
Our Lady of Guadalupe, 60-61
Mexico City, Mexico
captured by General Scott, 227
Michigan (mĭsh′ĭ·găn), 174, 219, 220
Michigan Territory, 220
Microscope (mī′krȯ·skōp), 332
Middle Colonies, 114-122
Dutch in the, 90-93, 95, 96, 115
life in the, 115-116, 130-133
Swedes in the, 94-96
Midway Islands (mĭd′wā), 317, 318
Military bases, *see* Bases, military
Mill-race (mĭl′rās′), 235
Mills, 321
Miners (mīn′ẽrz), 303
coal, 322
Minnesota (mĭn′ĕ·sō′tȧ), 278
admitted into the Union, 222
Minuit (mĭn′ŭ·ĭt), Peter
buys Manhattan, 92
in New Sweden, 94
Minute Men (mĭn′ĭt), 162, 163
Miraflores Locks (mĭr′ȧ·flōr′ĕs), 317
Missionaries, 6
See also under names of, e.g., Father Jacques Marquette, Saint Isaac Jogues, etc.
Missionary Sisters of the Sacred Heart, 364
Missions (mĭsh′ŭnz)
California, 231-233, 234
Indian life at, 232-234
Spanish, 65
Mississippi (mĭs′ĭ·sĭp′ĭ), 283
admitted into the Union, 220
settled by cotton farmers, 219

Mississippi River, 146, 153, 173, 194-195, 222
discovered by De Soto, 63, 83
explored by Marquette, 83-85
mouth reached by LaSalle, 86-87
Missouri (mĭ·zōō′rĭ), 240
admitted into the Union, 222
Missouri (ship), 358
Missouri Compromise, 272-273, 278
Missouri River
exploration, 197
Missouri Territory, 220
Mobile (mȯ·bēl′), Alabama, 211
"Model T" Ford, 330
Mohawk River (mō′hôk), 170
Mohawk Valley, 170
Monitor (mŏn′ĭ·tẽr) (warship), 286
Monmouth (mŏn′mŭth), battle of, 174
Monroe (mŭn·rō′), James, 203, 207
Monroe Doctrine, the, 206
Montana (mŏn·tăn′ȧ), 303
Montcalm (mŏnt·käm′), General Louis de, 151
Monterey (mŏn′tĕ·rā′), battle of, 227
Monterey Bay, 231, 235
Montezuma (mŏn′tĕ·zōō′mȧ), 58-59
Montgomery (mŏn(t)·gŭm′ẽr·ĭ), Alabama
Confederate States of America formed at, 282
Montreal (mŏn′trė·ȯl′), Canada, 77, 170
Moors (mōōrz)
Spain's war with the, 40
Morse (môrs), Samuel, 258, 326
Mother M. Angela, 289
Mother E. A. Seton (sē′t′n), 363-364
Mother F. X. Cabrini (kȧ·brē′nė), 364-366
Motion picture machine, first, 326
Mount Suribachi (sōōr′ĭ·bä′chĭ), Iwo Jima, 357
Mount Vernon (vûr′nŭn), Virginia
Washington's home at, 176, 185, 190, 191, 209
Movable type, 34

N

Nagasaki (nä′gȧ′sä′kė), Japan
atom bomb dropped on, 358

ix

Napoleon Bonaparte (nȧ·pō′lė·ŭn bō′nȧ·pärt)
  sold Louisiana to U. S., 195
Nashville (năsh′vĭl), Tennessee, 210, 215
National Progressives (prȯ·grĕs′ĭvz), 342
National Road, 249
Natural resources (rė·sōrs′ĭz)
  saving, 341, 353
Near East, 21, 23-24
Nebraska (nė·brăs′kȧ)
  Kansas-Nebraska Act, 277
Negroes (nē′grōz)
  blamed for troubles in the South following the Civil War, 296
  vote given to, 295
  See also Slaves
"Nesters" (nĕs′tērz), 306
'Nevada (nė·văd′ȧ), 228, 303
New Amsterdam (ăm′stēr·dăm), 92, 95, 114, 115
New Deal, 352-354
New England, 170·
  Northmen visit, 17
  Pilgrims and Puritans in, 102-112
New France, 76-88
  loss of, 146-154
New Hampshire (hăm[p]′shēr)
  settling of, 111
New Jersey (jûr′zĭ)
  colony of, 118
  slavery prohibited in, 271
  Washington retreats across, 168-169
New Mexico, 228
  admitted into the Union, 307
New Mexico Territory, 273
New Netherland (nĕth′ēr·lănd), 92, 95, 114-116
  becomes New York, 114-115
New Orleans (ôr′lė·ănz), Louisiana, 195
  battle of, 205, 210
  founding of, 87
New Sweden (swē′d'n), 94, 121
New World
  discovered by Europeans, 42-43
  discovered by the "Indians," 12
New York, 90-94, 114-117
New York Bay, 174
New York City, New York
  America's largest and richest city, 255
  bought from the Indians, 92
  capital of the U. S., 186
  Clermont makes trip to Albany from, 252-253

electric street-cars first used in, 329
Washington driven from, 168
Washington takes oath of office in, 186
New York State Barge Canal (bärj), 255
Newark (nū′ērk), N. J., 118
Newfoundland (nū′fŭn[d]·lănd′)
  French in, 76
Nome (nōm), Alaska, 309
Normandy (nôr′măn·dĭ), France, 357
North America
  discovered, 12, 16-17, 42-43, 48
  "Indians" in, 8-13
  Northmen in, 14-18
North American martyrs, 80-81
North Atlantic Treaty Organization, 375
North Carolina (kăr′ȯ·lī·nȧ), 126
North Dakota (dȧ·kō′tȧ), 197
Northmen
  discover America, 14-18, 44-45
Northwest Territory, 174, 219
Nueces River (nu·ā′sĕs), 227

O

Oahu (ȯ·ä′hōō), Hawaii, 312
Oglethorpe (ō′g'l·thôrp), James
  founds Georgia, 127
Ohio (ȯ·hī′ō), 219
  admitted into the Union, 220
  Clark in, 173-174
Ohio River, 173, 194, 218, 219
Ohio Valley, 146, 147, 148, 149, 173
Oil, 323, 333, 341
  crude oil, 323
  first American oil well, 323
  refineries, 323
Oklahoma (ō′klȧ·hō′mȧ)
  admitted into the Union, 307
  settlers, 306-307
Oklahoma City, Oklahoma, 307
Olaf of Norway (ō′läf), King, 16
Ontario (ŏn·târ′ĭ·ō), Lake, 170
Orange, Fort, 92, 95
Oregon (ŏr′ė·gŭn), 259, 298
  admitted into the Union, 245
  Father of, 242-243
Oregon (battleship), 316
Oregon Country, the, 196, 197, 220, 229, 240-245
  claimed by Great Britain and the U. S., 243-244
  divided between Great Britain and the U. S., 244-245
  Father De Smet in, 244

Oregon Free Territory, 273
Oregon Trail, 240-241, 249, 259
Oriskany (ȯ·rĭs′kȧ·nĭ), 170
Our Lady of Fatima (făt′ĭ·mȧ), 376
Our Lady of Guadalupe (gwä′ dȧ·lōōp′), 60, 61, 65
Our Lord, 21, 22, 24

P

Pacific Ocean (pȧ·sĭf′ĭk)
  discovered, 50
  Magellan and, 51-52
Pago Pago (päng′ō päng′ō), 317
Panama (păn′ȧ·mȯ), 236, 316
  Balboa crosses, 50
  Isthmus of, 236, 316
  Republic of, 317
Panama Canal, 316-317, 318, 340
Panama Canal Zone, 316
Papoose, 8
Paris Peace Conference (1919), 348
Parker (pär′kēr), Captain John, 163
Parliament (pär′lĭ·mĕnt), 156, 157, 158, 159, 161
Passaic River (pȧ·sā′ĭk), 118
Patroons, 92
Paulus Hook (pô′lŭs), battle at, 174
Pearl Harbor, 312, 356, 357
Pedro Miguel Locks (pā′drō mė·gĕl′), 316, 317
Penn, William, 118, 119-121
Pennsylvania (pĕn′sĭl·vā′nĭ·ȧ)
  colony of, 119-121
  "Dutch," 120
  life in, 130-133
Pensacola (pĕn′sȧ·kō′lȧ), Florida, 211
Perry, Oliver Hazard (hăz′ērd), 204
Persecution, religious, 102-103, 108, 119
Pershing (pûr′shĭng), General John J., 347
Peru (pė·rōō)
  history of, 63
Petroleum (pė·trō′lė·ŭm), 323, 333, 341
Philadelphia (fĭl′ȧ·dĕl′fĭ·ȧ), Pennsylvania, 170, 172, 174
  capital of the U. S., 190
  Constitutional Convention held in, 178
  First Continental Congress met at, 161
  laid out, 120, 121

x

Philippine Islands (fĭl′ĭ·pēn), 51, 313, 314, 318
  captured by Japan in World War II, 356
  independence granted to, 314
Phonograph (fō′nō·gràf)
  invented by Edison, 327
Picture stories
  Alaska today, 310-311
  astrolabe, the, 34
  Atlantic Cable, the, 259
  aviation, the story of, 331
  Cabrini, Saint Frances Xavier, 364
  Catholic schools, our, 367
  chemistry, the wonderland of, 332
  Civil War, the, 288-289
  coal mining, 322
  colonial life, 66, 111, 132-133, 154
  De Smet, Father Peter, S.J., 244
  Edison, Thomas—the great inventor, 326-327
  English colonial life, 111, 132-133
  Far East, the wonders of the, 30
  Ferdinand, Spanish colonist, 66
  Ford, Henry, 330
  French colonial life, 154
  fur trade in New York, the, 92-93
  Gallitzin, Father Demetrius, 362
  government, the three branches of the, 181
  Gutenberg, John, 34
  Howe, Elias, and the sewing machine, 264
  Indians, gifts of the American, 12
  iron and steel, 324-325
  Jean, a French colonist, 154
  Kateri Tekakwitha, 81
  life in the English colonies, 111, 132-133, 154
  life in a French colony, 154
  life in a Spanish colony, 66
  McCormick, Cyrus Hall, and the reaper, 263
  Mexican War, the, 228
  mining coal, 322
  Monroe Doctrine, the, 206
  Morse, Samuel, F.B., 258
  Mother Seton, 364
  Panama Canal, the, 316-317
  Paris Peace Conference of 1919, the, 348
  Paul, an English colonist, 111
  radio and telephone, the, 328
  railroads, the story of, 256
  reaper, Cyrus Hall McCormick and the, 263
  sailors, 34
  Saint Frances Xavier Cabrini, 364
  schools, our Catholic, 367
  Seton, Mother, 364
  sewing machine, Elias Howe and the, 264
  Spanish colonial life, 66
  Spanish-American War, the, 314
  steel and iron, 324-325
  tariff question, the, 213
  telephone and radio, the, 328
  Whitney, Eli, and his inventions, 262
  World War I, 346
  World War II, 357
Pike, Zebulon (zĕb′ụ·lŭn pīk), 198
Pike's Peak (pīks pēk),
  discovered, 198
  gold discovered near, 303
Pilgrims (pĭl′grĭmz), 102-107
Pipelines (pīp′līnz), 323
Pirates
  war against, 201
Pitcairn (pĭt′kârn), Major John, 163
Pitt (pĭt), William, 150
Pitt, Fort, 150
Pittsburgh (pĭts′bûrg), Pennsylvania, 173
Pius VII (pī′ŭs), Pope, 201
Pius XII, Pope, 61
Pizarro (pĭ·zär′ō), Francisco conquers Peru, 63
Plantations
  life on Southern, 138-140
Planters, Southern, 126, 138-140
Plymouth Colony (plĭm′ŭth)
  Pilgrims found, 105-107
Pocahontas (pō′ká·hŏn′tàs), 70, 71
Political parties
  first, 188-189
  See also names of parties
Polk (pōk), James, 227
Polo (pō′lō), Marco, 28-31, 43
Ponce de Leon (pôn′thā thå là·ôn′)
  discovers Florida, 64
Pony Express, 260, 329
Portage (pōr′tĭj), explained, 84
Portolá, Captain Don Gaspar de (gäs·pär då pôr′tô·lä′), 230, 231
Potomac River (pô·tō′măk), 190
Powhatan (pou′há·tăn′), Chief, 70

Prince Henry of Portugal, 32-35, 36
Princeton (prĭns′tŭn), New Jersey, 170
  battle of, 169, 170
Princeton University, 344
Printing, 20, 34, 39
Printing press, 34
Privateers (prī′và·tẽrz′), 171
Prospectors (prŏs′pĕk·tẽrz), 303
Providence (prŏv′ĭ·děns), R. I.
  founding of, 109
Protestants (prŏt′ĕs·tăntz), 102, 103
Pueblo, 64
Puerto Rico (pwĕr′tụ rē′kō), 314, 318
Pulaski, Casimir (kăz′ĭ·mĭr pụ·läs′kĭ), 175
Pure Food and Drug Law, 340
Puritan Church, 135, 137
Puritans (pū′rĭ·tănz), 107-108, 366

Q

Quakers (kwāk′ẽrz), 119
Quebec (kwê·běk′),
  Battle of, 150-151
  settlement of, 78

R

Radio (rā′dĭ·ō), beginning of, 328
Railroads, 255, 256, 257, 259, 261, 329, 332, 333
Raleigh (rô′lĭ), Sir Walter, 126
Randolph, Edmund (ĕd′mŭnd răn′dŏlf), 186, 187
Reaper (rēp′ẽr), 263
Reconstruction Act (rē′kŏn·strŭk′shŭn), 295
Refineries (rê·fīn′ẽr·ĭz), oil, 323
Relief (rê·lēf′), after World War II, 374
Religion, freedom of, see Freedom of religion
Republican Party (rê·pŭb′lĭ·kăn)
  opposed to spread of slavery, 278, 282
Reservations (rěz′ẽr·vā′shŭnz), Indian, 299-300, 306
Revere (rê·vẽr), Paul, 162
Revolutionary War (rěv′ô·lū′shŭn·ẽr′ĭ), see War for Independence
Rhode Island (rōd ī′lănd), 179
  Roger Williams founds, 109

xi

Richmond (rĭch′mŭnd), Virginia
 capital of the Confederacy, 284
 captured during Civil War, 290
Rio Grande River (rē′ō grănd′), 227, 228
River of Doubt, 342
Road(s)
 corduroy, 248
 Cumberland, 249
 first, in U. S., 247-248, 259
 National, 249
Rock Island steam train, 256
Rockefeller (rŏk′ĕ·fĕl′ēr), John D., 333
Rocky Mountains, 197, 260
 search for gold and silver in, 303
 "the Apostle of the Rockies," 244
Rolfe (rŏlf), John, 71
Roosevelt (rō′zĕ·vĕlt), Franklin D.
 as President, 352-358, 370
 Assistant Secretary of the Navy, 350
 cousin of Theodore Roosevelt, 350
 death of, 358, 371
 early life of, 350
 fourth term as President, 358
 Governor of N. Y., 352
 New Deal and, 352-354
 polio victim, 351
 second term as President, 354
 third term as President, 355
Roosevelt, Theodore (thē′ō·dōr),
 as President, 316, 338, 339-341
 Assistant Secretary of the Navy, 339-350
 cousin of Franklin D. Roosevelt, 350
 death of, 342-343
 defeated in election of 1912, 342, 345
 early life of, 338-339
 elected Vice-President, 339
 exploring expedition in Brazil, 342
 hunting trip in Africa, 342
 in Spanish-American War, 314, 339, 342
 life of, after serving as President, 342
Roosevelt Dam, 341
Roosevelt River, 342
Rough Riders, 314, 339
Rubber, 332
Russia (rŭsh′a)
 Alaska purchased from, 310
 Communism and, 372-376

Oregon claimed by, 243
World War I, 345

S

Sacajawea (săk′a·ja·wē′a), the Bird Woman, 197
Sacramento (săk′ra·měn′tō), California, 260
Sailors, 18
 new helps for, 34
 Northmen as, 14-15, 16, 18
 Prince Henry's, 32-37
St. Augustine (sānt ô′gŭs·tēn), Fla., 64
Saint Frances Xavier Cabrini, 364, 366
Saint Francis Xavier, 46
St. Ignace Mission (sānt ĭg′nas), 82, 85
St. Joseph (jō′zĕf), Missouri, 260
St. Lawrence River, 170
 discovery of, 77, 79
St. Leger (sānt lĕ′jēr), General Barry, 170
St. Louis, Missouri, 196
St. Malo fishermen (săN ma′lō′), 76, 77
St. Mary's College and Seminary (Baltimore), 362
Salem (sā′lĕm)
 Puritans come to, 107
Samoa Islands, see American Samoa
Samoset (săm′ō·sĕt), 106
Sampson (sămp′s'n), William T., 314
San Antonio (săn ăn·tō′nĭ·ō), Texas, 225
San Diego (săn′ dĭ·ā′gō), California, 230, 231
San Diego Bay, 236
San Francisco (săn′ frăn·sĭs′kō), California
 United Nations formed at, 371
San Francisco Bay, 231
San Jacinto (săn′ ja·sĭn′tō), battle at, 226
San Juan Hill (săn wän′), 314, 339
San Salvador (săn săl′va·dôr), 43
Santa Anna, General Antonio López de (än·tō′nyō lō′pas da sän′tä ä′nä), 225, 226, 228
Santa Fe Trail (săn′ta fā′), 249
Santa Maria (săn′ta ma·rē′a), the, 41, 42
Santiago (săn′tĭ·ä′gō), Cuba, 314
Saratoga (săr′a·tō′ga), New York, 170
 battle at, 170, 174

Savannah (sa·văn′a), Georgia
 captured by British, 175
 captured by Sherman, 288
"Scalawags" (skăl′a·wăgz), 295, 296
Schley (slī), Winfield S., 314
Schneider (shnī′dēr), Father Theodore, 118
Schools
 Catholic, in the United States, 366-367
 for sailors, 32-33
 Southern, 140
Scott, Dred (drĕd skŏt), 278
Scott, Fort, 211
Scott, Winfield (wĭn′fĕld), 227, 228
Second Continental Congress, 164, 165, 167, 174, 194
Security Council (United Nations), 372
Self-government, 137. See also Assemblies and Government
Seminole Indians (sĕm′ĭ·nōl), 211
Senate
 origin of, 180
Serapis (sĕ·rā′pĭs) (British warship), 172
Serra, Father Junípero (hōō·nē′pa·rō sĕr′rä), 65, 230, 231-232, 234
Seton (sē′t'n), Elizabeth Ann, 363-364
Seton, William Magee (ma·gē′), 363
Settlers
 Dutch, 90-94, 114-116, 120
 English, 68-74, 102-112, 118-120, 122, 124-129
 French, 76-88
 German, 120-121
 Swedish, 94, 95, 121
Seward (sū′ērd), William H., 310
"Seward's Icebox," 310
Sewing machine, 264
Shawnee Indians (shô·nē′), 217-218
Sherman (shûr′man), General William T., 228, 286, 288, 290
Shipbuilders, New England, 136
Sioux Indians (sōō), 300
Sisters of Charity, 364
Sisters of the Holy Cross, 289
Sitting Bull, Chief, 300
Slavery, 73, 136, 139, 268-279
 abolished by 13th Amendment, 290
Abolitionists, 274
 bitter feeling over, 274

xii

Compromise of 1850, 273, 276
  dies out in the North, 270-271
  Douglas' attitude toward, 282
  Dred Scott decision, 278
  Emancipation Proclamation, 289
  importance of, in the South, 269
  in territories, 271-272, 273, 289
  Kansas-Nebraska Act, 277
  Lincoln's attitude toward, 282
  Missouri Compromise, 272-273, 278
  Republicans oppose spread of, 278, 282
  Underground Railway, 275
Slaves, 268-279
  freed, 289, 292
  in Texas, 224
  life of, 269-270
  See also Negroes
Sloat (slōt), Commodore John Drake, 235
Smith, Alfred E., 351, 352
Smith, Captain John, 69-71, 105
Smith, Jedediah (jĕd'ê·dī'á), 234
Snorri (snôr'rĭ)
  first American-born white child, 17
Social Security Act, 354
Society for the Propagation of the Faith (prŏp'á·gā'shŭn), 366
South, the
  after the Civil War, 292-297
South America, 206
South Carolina (kăr'ô·līná), 209
  leaves the Union, 282
  settlement of, 126
  tariff dispute, 213-215, 275
Southern Colonies, 68-74, 124-129
Southern Trail, 249
Spain (spān), 171, 206, 222, 223
  California claimed by, 230
  Florida purchased from, 211
  gifts of, to the New World, 64-65, 66
  Oregon claimed by, 243
Spanish Cession (sĕsh'ŭn), 220
Spanish-American War, 313-314, 339, 342, 370
Spanish settlements, 58-66
  in California, 65
  in Mexico, 58-62
  in Peru, 63
  in the Southwest, 64-65
  in the United States, 63-65
Spice, 24, 25
Squanto (skwŏn'tō), 106
Squaws, 8, 125

"Spoils system" (spoilz), 213
Stagecoaches (stāj'kōch'ĭz), 249, 256, 260, 329
Stamp Act, 156-158
  repealed, 158
Stamp Act Congress, 158
Standard Oil Company, 333
Stanwix (stăn'wĭks), Fort, 170
"Star-Spangled Banner, The," 204
State government, 180, 181
Steam engine
  invented, 252, 320, 329
  uses, 321
Steamboats, 252-253, 321
Steamships, 253, 321, 322
Steel, 324-325
Stephenson (stē'vĕn·sŭn), John, 256
Steuben, Baron von (vŏn stū'bĕn), 175
Stockton (stŏk'tŭn), Commodore R. F., 235
Stony Point, battle at, 174
Stowe, Harriet Beecher (bē'chēr stō), 274
Street-cars, electric, 329
Stuyvesant (stī'vĕ·s'nt), Governor Peter, 114-115
Submarines, 346
  German, 345, 346, 355
Sumter (sŭm'tēr), Fort, 283
Suwanee (sōō·wô'nê), Florida, 211
Swedes
  Delaware settled by, 94, 95, 121

T

Taft (tăft), William Howard, 342, 345
Tank, armored, 346
Tariff (tăr'ĭf)
  defined, 213
  reasons for, 213
  South Carolina and the, 213-215, 275
"Taxation without representation," 157, 159
Taxes
  after Civil War, 295
  during World War I, 348
  in colonial days, 156-161
Taylor, Zachary (zăk'á·rĭ tā'lēr), 227-228
Tea
  tax on, 159, 160
Tekakwitha, see Kateri Tekakwitha

Telegraph
  improved by Edison, 327
  invented, 258-259
Telephone
  invented, 328
Television, 328
"Tenderfoot," 339
Tennessee (tĕn'ĕ·sē')
  admitted into the Union, 220
  first settlements in, 217
Tepees, 11
Territories, see names of territories
Texas (tĕk'săs), 222-229
  admitted into the Union, 226
  becomes independent, 225-226
  cattle raising in, 304
  discovered, 87
  early settlers, 222-223
  Father of, 223
  trouble with Mexico over, 224-229
Texas Annexation (ăn'ĕk·sā'shŭn) (1845), 229
Ticonderoga (tī'kŏn·dēr·ō'gá), Fort, 163, 164
Tin cans, 325
Titusville (tī'tŭs·vĭl), Pennsylvania, 323
Tobacco (tō·băk'ō)
  in the South, 72, 126, 138
Toleration Act, 126
Tollgates (tōl'gāts'), 248
"Tolls" (tōlz), 248
Tom Thumb (thŭm) (locomotive), 257
Tomahawk, 9
Trade, 23, 24, 25, 26, 30-31, 138
Transportation (trăns'pôr·tā'shŭn)
  air, 331
  canals, 254-255, 259
  defined, 247
  early travel by water, 246-247
  railroads, 257, 259, 261
  roads, 247-249, 259
  steamboats and steamships, 252-253, 321
Travis (trăv'ĭs), Colonel William, 225
Treaty of Paris (1763), 151
Treaty of Paris (1783), 178
Trenton (trĕn't'n), New Jersey, 170
  battle of, 169, 170
Triple Alliance (á·lī'ăns), 346
Triple Entente (äN'täNt'), 346
Tripoli (trĭp'ô·lĭ)
  war against pirates from, 201
"Trips," 322

xiii

Truman (trōō′măn), Harry S., 371
Turkey (tûr′kĭ)
 World War I, 345
Type, movable, 34

U

U-boat, 346
Uncle Tom's Cabin (book), 274
Underground Railway, 275
Union Pacific Railroad, 261
United Nations, 358, 370, 371-373, 374, 375
 charter, 371
 Conference at San Francisco, 371
 headquarters, 372
 Security Council, 372
 veto power in, 372
 weakness of, 372
United States
 birth of, 165
 in 1783, 229
 in 1819, 220
 Spaniards in, 63-65
United States Military Academy, 283
United States Steel Corporation, 333
Utah (ū′tä), 228
Utah Territory, 273

V

Vacuum cleaner (vak′ū·ŭm), 327
Valley Forge (fôrj), Pennsylvania, 170, 175
 Washington at, 171
Van Buren (văn bū′rĕn), Martin, 215
Vancouver (văn·kōō′vẽr), Fort, 241, 242
Vanderbilt, Cornelius (kôr·nēl′yŭs văn′dẽr·bĭlt), 333
Venice (vĕn′ĭs)
 merchants of, 25, 28
Vermont (vẽr·mŏnt′)
 slavery prohibited in, 271
Verrazano (vär′rä·tsä′nô), Giovanni da
 explores North America, 76
Vespucci, Amerigo (ä′mä·rē′gô vĕs·pōō′chĕ), 85
 writes about America, 49
Veto power (vē′tō) (United Nations), 372

Vicksburg (vĭks′bûrg), Mississippi
 surrender of, 286, 287, 289
Village life in New England, 134
Victoria (vĭk·tō′rĭ·á), the, 51
Vincennes (vĭn·sĕnz′), Fort, 173, 174
Vinland (vĭn′lănd)
 Northmen visit, 17-18
Virgin Islands (vûr′jĭn), 318
Virginia (vẽr·jĭn′yá), 68-74, 209
 gives Confederate States a capital and a great general, 284
Viscaíno, Don Sebastian (sā′bäs·tyän′ vēth′kä·ē′nô), 231
Voting, in colonies, 137

W

Wabash River (wô′băsh), 173
Waikiki Beach (wī′kĭ·kē′), Hawaii, 312
Wake Island (wāk), 317, 318, 356
Wampum, 9
War between the States, *see* Civil War, the
War for Independence, 162-165, 167-176, 210, 219, 324, 329, 361
"War Hawks," 203
War of 1812, 203-205, 210, 321, 338
Warm Springs, Georgia, 351
Washing machine, first, 327
Washington (wŏsh′ĭng·tŭn)
 admitted into the Union, 245
Washington, D. C.
 captured by British, 204
 founded, 190
Washington, George, 128
 as Commander-in-Chief, 164-165, 167-171, 174, 175, 176, 185, 324
 as President, 185-191, 361
 at Valley Forge, 171
 British driven from Boston by, 164-165
 death of, 191
 driven from New York City, 167-168
 First Continental Congress, 162
 his cabinet, 186-188
 in French and Indian War, 146, 147, 148, 149, 150
 leaves the army, 176
 President of Constitutional Convention, 179, 185

retreats across New Jersey, 168-169
 second term, 190
 takes oath of office, 186
Watt (wŏt), James, 252, 320
Wayne (wān), "Mad Anthony," 174
West, the
 settlement of, 298-307
West Point, 283, 284, 287
 Arnold offers to sell fort to British, 174
West Virginia, 218, 219
Whigs (hwĭgz), 278
White, Father Andrew, 124, 125
Whitney, Eli (ē′lĭ hwĭt′nĭ), 219, 262, 269
Wichita (wĭch′ĭ·tô), Kansas, 305
Wigwams (wĭg′wŏms), 11
Wilderness, 8-9
Wilderness Road, 219
William and Mary College, 193
Williams (wĭl′yămz), Roger, 109, 125
Williamsburg (wĭl′yămz·bûrg), Virginia, 193
Wilmington (wĭl′mĭng·tŭn), Del.
 founding of, 94
Wilson, Woodrow (wōōd′rō wĭl′s'n), 342, 344-348, 350, 358, 370
 death of, 348
 elected Governor of N. J., 344
Wineland (wĭn′lănd), 17-18
Winthrop (wĭn′thrŭp), Governor John, 107
Wisconsin (wĭs·kŏn′s'n), 174, 219, 220
Wolfe (wōōlf), General James, 150-151
Wood, Colonel Leonard, 313
World War I, 342, 345-348, 350, 370
World War II, 311, 354-358, 370, 373-374
 in Europe, 356-357
 U. S. entry into, 356
 victories in the Pacific, 356
Wright, Orville (ôr′vĭl rīt), 331
Wright, Wilbur (wĭl′bẽr), 331
Wyoming (wī·ō′mĭng), 228-229

Y

Yorktown (yôrk′toun), Virginia
 British surrender at, 175, 176, 188